/12

W9-BKP-400

SECOND EDITION

Linux
Pocket Guide

Daniel J. Barrett

O'REILLY®

Beijing · Cambridge · Farnham · Köln · Sebastopol · Tokyo

Linux Pocket Guide, Second Edition

by Daniel J. Barrett

Copyright © 2012 Daniel Barrett. All rights reserved.
Printed in the United States of America.

Published by O'Reilly Media, Inc., 1005 Gravenstein Highway North, Sebastopol, CA 95472.

O'Reilly books may be purchased for educational, business, or sales promotional use. Online editions are also available for most titles (*http://my.safari booksonline.com*). For more information, contact our corporate/institutional sales department: (800) 998-9938 or *corporate@oreilly.com*.

Editors: Mike Loukides and Andy Oram
Copyeditor: Rachel Monaghan
Production Editor: Melanie Yarbrough
Proofreader: Stacie Arellano
Indexer: Daniel Barrett
Cover Designer: Karen Montgomery
Interior Designer: David Futato
Illustrator: Robert Romano

| February 2004: | First Edition. |
| March 2012: | Second Edition. |

Revision History for the Second Edition:

2012-09-07	Fourth release
2012-12-21	Fifth release
2013-06-07	Sixth release
2013-08-16	Seventh release
2013-10-25	Eighth release

See *http://oreilly.com/catalog/errata.csp?isbn=9781449316693* for release details.

Nutshell Handbook, the Nutshell Handbook logo, and the O'Reilly logo are registered trademarks of O'Reilly Media, Inc. *Linux Pocket Guide, Second Edition*, the cover image of a roper, and related trade dress are trademarks of O'Reilly Media, Inc.

Many of the designations used by manufacturers and sellers to distinguish their products are claimed as trademarks. Where those designations appear in this book, and O'Reilly Media, Inc., was aware of a trademark claim, the designations have been printed in caps or initial caps.

While every precaution has been taken in the preparation of this book, the publisher and author assume no responsibility for errors or omissions, or for damages resulting from the use of the information contained herein.

ISBN: 978-1-449-31669-3

[LSI]

1382382951

Contents

Linux Pocket Guide

Welcome to Linux! If you're a new user, this book can serve as a quick introduction, as well as a guide to common and practical commands. If you have Linux experience, feel free to skip the introductory material.

What's in This Book?

This book is a short guide, *not a comprehensive reference*. We cover important, useful aspects of Linux so you can work productively. We do not, however, present every single command and every last option (our apologies if your favorite was omitted), nor delve into detail about operating system internals. Short, sweet, and essential, that's our motto.

We focus on *commands*, those pesky little words you type on a command line to tell a Linux system what to do. Here's an example command that counts lines of text in a file, *myfile*:

```
wc -l myfile
```

We'll cover the most important Linux commands for the average user, such as ls (list files), grep (search for text in a file), amarok (play audio files), and df (measure free disk space). We touch only briefly on graphical windowing environments like GNOME and KDE, each of which could fill a Pocket Guide by itself.

We've organized the material by function to provide a concise learning path. For example, to help you view the contents of a file, we introduce all file-viewing commands together: `cat` for short text files, `less` for longer ones, `od` for binary files, `acro read` for PDF files, and so on. Then we explain each command in turn, briefly presenting its common uses and options.

We assume you have an account on a Linux system and know how to log in with your username and password. If not, speak with your system administrator, or if the system is your own, use the account created when you installed Linux.

What's Linux?

Linux is a popular, open source operating system that competes with Microsoft Windows and the Apple Macintosh. There are two ways to work with a Linux system:

- A graphical user interface with windows, icons, and mouse control.
- A command-line interface, called the *shell*, for typing and running commands like the preceding `wc`.

Windows and Mac OS computers can be operated by command line as well (Windows with its `cmd` and PowerShell command tools, and OS X with its Terminal application), but most of their users can survive without typing commands. On Linux, however, the shell is critical. If you use Linux without the shell, you are missing out.

What's a Distro?

Linux is extremely configurable and includes thousands of programs. As a result, different varieties of Linux have arisen to serve different needs and tastes. They all share certain core components but may look different and include different programs and files. Each variety is called a *distro* (short for "distribution"). Popular distros include Ubuntu Linux, Red Hat

Enterprise Linux, Slackware, Mint, and more. This book covers core material that should apply to every distro.

What's a Command?

A Linux command typically consists of a *program name* followed by *options* and *arguments*, typed within a shell, like this:

```
$ wc -l myfile
```

The program name (wc, the "word count" program) refers to a program somewhere on disk that the shell will locate and run. Options, which usually begin with a dash, affect the behavior of the program. In the preceding command, the -l option tells wc to count lines rather than words. The argument myfile specifies the file that wc should read and process. The leading dollar sign ($) is a *prompt* from the shell, indicating that it is waiting for your command.

Commands can have multiple options and arguments. Options may be given individually:

```
$ wc -l -w myfile          Two individual options
```

or combined behind a single dash:

```
$ wc -lw myfile            Same as -l -w
```

though some programs are quirky and do not recognize combined options. Multiple arguments are also OK:

```
$ wc -l myfile1 myfile2     Count lines in two files
```

Options are not standardized. The same option letter (say, -l) may have different meanings to different programs: in wc -l it means "lines of text," but in ls -l it means "longer output." In the other direction, two programs might use different options to mean the same thing, such as -q for "run quietly" versus -s for "run silently."

Likewise, arguments are not standardized, unfortunately. They usually represent filenames for input or output, but they can be other things too, like directory names or regular expressions.

Commands can be more complex and interesting than a single program with options:

- Commands can run more than one program at a time, either in sequence (one program after another) or in a "pipeline" with the output of one command becoming the input of the next. Linux experts use pipelines all the time.

- The Linux command-line user interface—the *shell*—has a programming language built in. So instead of a command saying "run this program," it might say, "if today is Tuesday, run this program; otherwise, run another command six times for each file whose name ends in *.txt*."

Reading This Book

We'll describe many Linux commands in this book. Each description begins with a standard heading about the command; Figure 1 shows one for the ls (list files) command. This heading demonstrates the general usage in a simple format:

```
ls [options] [files]
```

which means you'd type "ls" followed, if you choose, by options and then filenames. You wouldn't type the square brackets "[" and "]": they just indicate their contents are optional; and words in italics mean you have to fill in your own specific values, like names of actual files. If you see a vertical bar between options or arguments, perhaps grouped by parentheses:

```
(file | directory)
```

This indicates choice: you may supply either a filename or directory name as an argument.

The special heading also includes six properties of the command printed in black (supported) or gray (unsupported):

stdin

The command reads from standard input, i.e., your keyboard, by default. See "Input and Output" on page 12.

ls		stdin	**stdout**	- file	-- opt	--help	--version

```
ls [options] [files]
```

Figure 1. Standard command heading

stdout

> The command writes to standard output, i.e., your screen, by default. See "Input and Output" on page 12.

- file

> When given a dash (-) argument in place of an input filename, the command reads from standard input; and likewise, if the dash is supplied as an output filename, the command writes to standard output. For example, the following wc command line reads the files *file1* and *file2*, then standard input, then *file3*:

```
$ wc file1 file2 - file3
```

-- opt

> If you supply the command-line option "--" it means "end of options": anything appearing later on the command line is not an option. This is sometimes necessary to operate on a file whose name begins with a dash, which otherwise would be (mistakenly) treated as an option. For example, if you have a file named *-foo*, the command wc -foo will fail because -foo will be treated as an (invalid) option. wc -- -foo works. If a command does not support "--", you can prepend the current directory path "./" to the filename so the dash is no longer the first character:

```
$ wc ./-foo
```

--help

> The option --help makes the command print a help message explaining proper usage, then exit.

--version

> The option --version makes the command print its version information and exit.

Shell prompts

Some commands in this book can be run successfully only by the *superuser*, a special user with permission to do anything on the system. In this case, we use a hash mark (#) as the shell prompt:

```
# superuser command goes here
```

Otherwise, we will use the dollar sign prompt, indicating an ordinary user:

```
$ ordinary command goes here
```

Keystrokes

Throughout the book, we use certain symbols to indicate keystrokes. Like many other Linux documents, we use the ^ symbol to mean "press and hold the Control (Ctrl) key," so for example, ^D (pronounced "control D") means "press and hold the Control key and type D." We also write ESC to mean "press the Escape key." Keys like Enter and the space bar should be self-explanatory.

Your friend, the echo command

In many of our examples, we'll print information to the screen with the echo command, which we'll formally describe in "Screen Output" on page 168. echo is one of the simplest commands: it merely prints its arguments on standard output, once those arguments have been processed by the shell.

```
$ echo My dog has fleas
My dog has fleas
$ echo My name is $USER          Shell variable USER
My name is smith
```

Getting Help

If you need more information than this book provides, there are several things you can do.

Run the man *command*

The man command displays an online manual page, or *manpage*, for a given program. For example, to learn about listing files with ls, run:

```
$ man ls
```

To search for manpages by keyword for a particular topic, use the -k option followed by the keyword:

```
$ man -k database
```

Run the info *command*

The info command is an extended, hypertext help system covering many Linux programs.

```
$ info ls
```

While info is running, some useful keystrokes are:

- To get help, type h
- To quit, type q
- To page forward and backward, use the space bar and Backspace keys
- To jump between hyperlinks, press TAB
- To follow a hyperlink, press Enter

If info has no documentation on a given program, it displays the program's manpage. For a listing of available documentation, type info by itself. To learn how to navigate the info system, type info info.

Use the --help *option (if any)*

Many Linux commands respond to the option --help by printing a short help message. Try:

```
$ ls --help
```

If the output is longer than the screen, pipe it into the less program to display it in pages (press q to quit):

```
$ ls --help | less
```

Examine the directory /usr/share/doc

> This directory contains supporting documents for many
> programs, usually organized by program name and ver-
> sion. For example, files for the text editor emacs, version
> 23, are likely found (depending on distro) in */usr/share/
> doc/emacs23*.

GNOME and KDE Help

> For help with GNOME or KDE, visit *http://www.gnome
> .org* or *http://www.kde.org*.

Distro-specific websites

> Most Linux distros have an official site that includes doc-
> umentation, discussion forums for questions and an-
> swers, and other resources. Simply enter the distro name
> (e.g., "Ubuntu") into any popular search engine to find its
> web site. You can also visit the web site for this book: *http:
> //shop.oreilly.com/product/0636920023029.do*.

Linux help sites

> Many web sites answer Linux questions, such as *http://
> www.linuxquestions.org*, *http://unix.stackexchange.com*,
> *http://www.linuxhelp.net*, and *http://www.linuxforums
> .org*.

Web search

> To decipher a specific Linux error message, enter the mes-
> sage into a web search engine, word for word, and you
> will likely find helpful results.

Linux: A First View

Linux has four major parts:

The kernel

> The low-level operating system, handling files, disks, net-
> working, and other necessities we take for granted. Most
> users rarely notice the kernel.

Supplied programs

> Thousands of programs for file manipulation, text editing,
> mathematics, web browsing, audio, video, computer

programming, typesetting, encryption, DVD burning... you name it.

The shell

A user interface for typing commands, executing them, and displaying the results. Linux has various shells: the Bourne shell, Korn shell, C shell, and others. This book focuses on bash, the Bourne-Again Shell, which is often the default for user accounts. However, all these shells have similar basic functions.

X

A graphical system that provides windows, menus, icons, mouse support, and other familiar GUI elements. More complex graphical environments are built on X; the most popular are KDE and GNOME. We'll discuss a few programs that open X windows to run.

This book focuses on the second and third parts: supplied programs and the shell.

The Graphical Desktop

When you log into a Linux system, you're likely to be greeted by a graphical desktop[1] like Figure 2, which contains:

- A main menu or taskbar. Depending on your distro and system settings, this might be at the top, bottom, or side of the screen.

- Desktop icons representing the computer, a folder representing your home directory for personal files, a trash can, and more.

- Icons to run applications, such as the Firefox web browser and the Thunderbird email program.

- Controls for opening and closing windows and running multiple desktops at once.

---

1. Unless you're logging in remotely over the network, in which case you'll see just a command prompt, waiting for you to type a command.

- A clock and other small, informational icons.

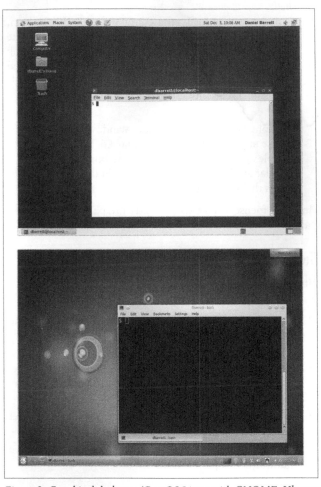

Figure 2. Graphical desktops (CentOS Linux with GNOME, Ubuntu with KDE). Desktops can look wildly different, depending on your distro and system settings.

Linux systems have several graphical interfaces, the most common being GNOME and KDE. Identify yours by clicking your system's equivalent of a main menu or start menu and looking for the words GNOME, KDE, Kubuntu (KDE on Ubuntu Linux), or similar.

Running a Shell

The icons and menus in GNOME and KDE are, for some users, the primary way to work with Linux. This is fine for simple tasks like reading email and browsing the Web. Nevertheless, the true power of Linux lies beneath this graphical interface, in the shell.

To get the most out of Linux, take the time to become proficient with the shell. (That's what this book is all about.) It might initially be more difficult than icons and menus, but once you're used to it, the shell is quite easy to use and *very* powerful.

To run a shell within GNOME, KDE, or any other graphical interface for Linux, you need to open a *shell window*: a window with a shell running in it. Figure 2 shows two shell windows with "$" shell prompts, awaiting your commands. Look through your system menus for an application to do this. Typical menu items are Terminal, xterm, gnome-terminal, konsole, and uxterm.

Don't confuse the window program (like konsole) with the shell running inside it. The window is just a container—possibly with fancy features of its own—but the shell is what prompts you for commands and runs them.

If you're not running a graphical interface—say, you're logging in remotely over the network, or directly over an attached terminal—a shell will run immediately when you log in. No shell window is required.

This was just a quick introduction. We'll discuss more details in "The Shell" on page 22, and cover more powerful constructs in "Programming with Shell Scripts" on page 195.

Input and Output

Most Linux commands accept input and produce output. Input can come from files or from *standard input*, which is usually your keyboard. Likewise, output is written to files or to *standard output*, which is usually your shell window or screen. Error messages are treated specially and displayed on *standard error*, which also is usually your screen but kept separate from standard output.[2] Later we'll see how to *redirect* standard input, output, and error to and from files or pipes. But let's get our vocabulary straight. When we say a command "reads," we mean from standard input unless we say otherwise. And when a command "writes" or "prints," we mean on standard output, unless we're talking about computer printers.

Users and Superusers

Linux is a multiuser operating system: multiple people can use a single Linux computer at the same time. On a given computer, each user is identified by a unique *username*, like "smith" or "funkyguy," and owns a (reasonably) private part of the system for doing work. There is also a special user named *root*—the *superuser*—who has the privileges to do anything at all on the system. Ordinary users are restricted: though they can run most programs, in general they can modify only the files they own. The superuser, on the other hand, can create, modify, or delete any file and run any program.

To become the superuser, you needn't log out and log back in; just run the su command (see "Becoming the Superuser" on page 138) and provide the superuser password:

```
$ su -l
Password: *******
#
```

---

2. For example, you can capture standard output in a file and still have standard error messages appear on screen.

The superuser prompt (#) indicates that you're ready to run superuser commands. Alternatively, run the sudo command (if your system is configured to use it), which executes a single command as the superuser, then returns control to the original user:

```
$ sudo ls /private/secrets        View a protected directory
Password: *******
secretfile1    secretfile2        It worked!
$
```

The Filesystem

To make use of any Linux system, you need to be comfortable with Linux files and *directories* (a.k.a. folders). In a "windows and icons" system, the files and directories are obvious on screen. With a command-line system like the Linux shell, the same files and directories are still present but are not constantly visible, so at times you must remember which directory you are "in" and how it relates to other directories. You'll use shell commands like cd and pwd to "move" between directories and keep track of where you are.

Let's cover some terminology. As we've said, Linux files are collected into directories. The directories form a hierarchy, or *tree*, as in Figure 3: one directory may contain other directories, called *subdirectories*, which may themselves contain other files and subdirectories, and so on, into infinity. The topmost directory is called the *root directory* and is denoted by a slash (/).[3]

We refer to files and directories using a "names and slashes" syntax called a *path*. For instance, this path:

/one/two/three/four

refers to the root directory /, which contains a directory called *one*, which contains a directory *two*, which contains a directory

---

3. In Linux, *all* files and directories descend from the root. This is unlike Windows or DOS, in which different devices are accessed by drive letters.

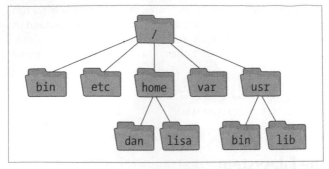

Figure 3. A Linux filesystem (partial). The root folder is at the top. The "dan" folder's full path is /home/dan.

three, which contains a final file or directory, *four*. If a path begins with the root directory, it's called an *absolute* path, and if not, it's a *relative* path. More on this in a moment.

Whenever you are running a shell, that shell is working "in" some directory (in an abstract sense). More technically, your shell has a *current working directory*, and when you run commands in that shell, they operate relative (there's that word again) to the directory. More specifically, if you refer to a relative file path in that shell, it is relative to your current working directory. For example, if your shell is "in" the directory */one/two/three*, and you run a command that refers to a file *myfile*, then the file is really */one/two/three/myfile*. Likewise, a relative path *a/b/c* would imply the true path */one/two/three/a/b/c*.

Two special directories are denoted . (a single period) and .. (two periods in a row). The former means your current directory, and the latter means your *parent* directory, one level above. So if your current directory is */one/two/three*, then . refers to this directory and .. refers to */one/two*.

You "move" your shell from one directory to another using the cd command:

```
$ cd /one/two/three
```

More technically, this command changes your shell's current working directory to be */one/two/three*. This is an absolute change (since the directory begins with "/"); of course you can make relative moves as well:

```
$ cd d                    Enter subdirectory d
$ cd ../mydir             Go up to my parent, then into directory mydir
```

File and directory names may contain most characters you expect: capital and lowercase letters,[4] numbers, periods, dashes, underscores, and most symbols (but not "/", which is reserved for separating directories). For practical use, however, avoid spaces, asterisks, parentheses, and other characters that have special meaning to the shell. Otherwise, you'll need to quote or escape these characters all the time. (See "Quoting" on page 29.)

Home Directories

Users' personal files are often found in /home (for ordinary users) or /root (for the superuser). Your home directory is typically /home/*your-username*: /home/smith, /home/jones, etc. There are several ways to locate or refer to your home directory.

cd

> With no arguments, the cd command returns you (i.e., sets the shell's working directory) to your home directory.

HOME *variable*

> The environment variable HOME (see "Shell variables" on page 25) contains the name of your home directory.
>
> ```
> $ echo $HOME          The echo command prints its arguments
> /home/smith
> ```

~

> When used in place of a directory, a lone tilde is expanded by the shell to the name of your home directory.
>
> ```
> $ echo ~
> /home/smith
> ```

---

4. Linux filenames are case-sensitive, so capital and lowercase letters are not equivalent.

When followed by a username (as in ~fred), the shell expands this string to be the user's home directory:

```
$ cd ~fred
$ pwd                    The "print working directory" command
/home/fred
```

System Directories

A typical Linux system has tens of thousands of system directories. These directories contain operating system files, applications, documentation, and just about everything *except* personal user files (which typically live in */home*).

Unless you're a system administrator, you'll rarely visit most system directories—but with a little knowledge you can understand or guess their purposes. Their names often contain three parts, which we'll call the scope, category, and application. (These are not standard terms, but they'll help you understand things.) For example, the directory */usr/local/share/emacs*, which contains local data for the emacs text editor, has scope */usr/local* (locally installed system files), category *share* (program-specific data and documentation), and application *emacs* (a text editor), shown in Figure 4. We'll explain these three parts, slightly out of order.

Figure 4. Directory scope, category, and application

Directory path part 1: category

A *category* tells you the types of files found in a directory. For example, if the category is *bin*, you can be reasonably assured that the directory contains programs. Common categories are:

Categories for programs

bin	Programs (usually binary files)
sbin	Programs (usually binary files) intended to be run by the superuser
lib	Libraries of code used by programs
libexec	Programs invoked by other programs, not usually by users; think "library of executable programs"

Categories for documentation

doc	Documentation
info	Documentation files for emacs's built-in help system
man	Documentation files (manual pages) displayed by the man program; the files are often compressed, or sprinkled with typesetting commands for man to interpret
share	Program-specific files, such as examples and installation instructions

Categories for configuration

etc	Configuration files for the system (and other miscellaneous stuff)
init.d	Configuration files for booting Linux
rc.d	Configuration files for booting Linux; also *rc1.d, rc2.d, ...*

Categories for programming

include	Header files for programming
src	Source code for programs

Categories for web files

cgi-bin	Scripts/programs that run on web pages
html	Web pages
public_html	Web pages, typically in users' home directories
www	Web pages

Categories for display

fonts	Fonts (surprise!)
X11	X window system files

Categories for hardware

dev	Device files for interfacing with disks and other hardware

media	Mount points: directories that provide access to disks
mnt	Mount points: directories that provide access to disks
misc	Mount points: directories that provide access to disks

Categories for runtime files

var	Files specific to this computer, created and updated as the computer runs
lock	Lock files, created by programs to say, "I am running"; the existence of a lock file may prevent another program, or another instance of the same program, from running or performing an action
log	Log files that track important system events, containing error, warning, and informational messages
mail	Mailboxes for incoming mail
run	PID files, which contain the IDs of running processes; these files are often consulted to track or kill particular processes
spool	Files queued or in transit, such as outgoing email, print jobs, and scheduled jobs
tmp	Temporary storage for programs and/or people to use
proc	Operating system state: see "Operating System Directories" on page 19

Directory path part 2: scope

The *scope* of a directory path describes, at a high level, the purpose of an entire directory hierarchy. Some common ones are:

/	System files supplied with Linux (pronounced "root")
/usr	More system files supplied with Linux (pronounced "user")
/usr/games	Games (surprise!)
/usr/local	System files developed "locally," either for your organization or your individual computer
/usr/X11R6	Files pertaining to the X window system

So for a category like *lib* (libraries), your Linux system might have directories */lib*, */usr/lib*, */usr/local/lib*, */usr/games/lib*, and */usr/X11R6/lib*.

There isn't a clear distinction between / and *usr* in practice, but there is a sense that / is "lower-level" and closer to the operating system. So */bin* contains fundamental programs like ls and cat, */usr/bin* contains a wide variety of applications supplied with your Linux distribution, and */usr/local/bin* contains programs your system administrator chose to install. These are not hard-and-fast rules but typical cases.

Directory path part 3: application

The application part of a directory path, if present, is usually the name of a program. After the scope and category (say, */usr/local/doc*), a program may have its own subdirectory (say, */usr/local/doc/myprogram*) containing files it needs.

Operating System Directories

Some directories support the Linux kernel, the lowest-level part of the Linux operating system.

/boot
> Files for booting the system. This is where the kernel lives, typically named */boot/vmlinuz*.

/lost+found
> Damaged files that were rescued by a disk recovery tool.

/proc
> Describes currently running processes; for advanced users.

The files in */proc* provide views into the running kernel and have special properties. They always appear to be zero sized, read-only, and dated now:

```
$ ls -l /proc/version
-r--r--r--  1 root    root    0 Oct  3 22:55 /proc/version
```

However, their contents magically contain information about the Linux kernel:

```
$ cat /proc/version
Linux version 2.6.32-71.el6.i686 ...
```

Files in */proc* are used mostly by programs, but feel free to explore them. Here are some examples:

/proc/ioports	A list of your computer's input/output hardware.
/proc/version	The operating system version. The uname command prints the same information.
/proc/uptime	System uptime, i.e., seconds elapsed since the system was last booted. Run the uptime command for a more human-readable result.
*/proc/**nnn***	Where *nnn* is a positive integer, information about the Linux process with process ID *nnn*.
/proc/self	Information about the current process you're running; a symbolic link to a */proc/nnn* file, automatically updated. Try `ls -l /proc/self` several times in a row: you'll see */proc/self* changing where it points.

File Protections

A Linux system may have many users with login accounts. To maintain privacy and security, most users can access only *some* files on the system, not all. This access control is embodied in two questions:

Who has permission?

>   Every file and directory has an *owner* who has permission to do anything with it. Typically the user who created a file is its owner, but relationships can be more complex.

>   Additionally, a predefined *group* of users may have permission to access a file. Groups are defined by the system administrator and are covered in "Group Management" on page 140.

>   Finally, a file or directory can be opened to *all users* with login accounts on the system. You'll also see this set of users called *the world* or simply *other*.

What kind of permission is granted?

>   File owners, groups, and the world may each have permission to *read*, *write* (modify), and *execute* (run) particular files. Permissions also extend to directories, which

users may read (access files within the directory), write (create and delete files within the directory), and execute (enter the directory with **cd**).

To see the ownership and permissions of a file, run:

```
$ ls -l myfile
-rw-r--r-- 1 smith smith   7384 Jan 04 22:40 myfile
```

To see the ownership and permissions of a directory, run:

```
$ ls -ld dirname
drwxr-x--- 3 smith smith   4096 Jan 08 15:02 dirname
```

In the output, the file permissions are the 10 leftmost characters, a string of **r** (read), **w** (write), **x** (execute), other letters, and dashes. For example:

```
-rwxr-x---
```

Here's what these letters and symbols mean.

Position	Meaning
1	File type: - = file, d = directory, l = symbolic link, p = named pipe, c = character device, b = block device
2–4	Read, write, and execute permissions for the file's owner
5–7	Read, write, and execute permissions for the file's group
8–10	Read, write, and execute permissions for all other users

So our example `-rwxr-x---` means a file that can be read, written, and executed by the owner, read and executed by the group, and not accessed at all by the rest of the world. We describe **ls** in more detail in "Basic File Operations" on page 36. To change the owner, group ownership, or permissions of a file, use the **chown**, **chgrp**, and **chmod** commands, respectively, as described in "File Properties" on page 59.

The Shell

In order to run commands on a Linux system, you'll need somewhere to type them. That "somewhere" is called the *shell*, which is Linux's command-line user interface: you type a command and press Enter, and the shell runs whatever program (or programs) you've requested. (See "Running a Shell" on page 11 to learn how to open a shell window.)

For example, to see who's logged in, you could execute this command in a shell:

```
$ who
silver     :0      Sep 23 20:44
byrnes     pts/0   Sep 15 13:51
barrett    pts/1   Sep 22 21:15
silver     pts/2   Sep 22 21:18
```

(The dollar sign is the shell prompt, which means the shell is ready to run a command.) A single command can also invoke several programs at the same time, and even connect programs together so they interact. Here's a command that redirects the output of the who program to become the input of the wc program, which counts lines of text in a file; the result is the number of lines in the output of who:

```
$ who | wc -l
4
```

telling you how many users are logged in.[5] The vertical bar, called a *pipe*, makes the connection between who and wc.

A shell is actually a program itself, and Linux has several. We focus on bash (the Bourne-Again Shell), located in */bin/bash*, which is usually the default in Linux distros.

---

5. Actually, how many interactive shells those users are running. If a user has two shells running, like the user silver in our example, he'll have two lines of output from who.

The Shell Versus Programs

When you run a command, it might invoke a Linux program (like who), or instead it might be a *built-in command*, a feature of the shell itself. You can tell the difference with the type command:

```
$ type who
who is /usr/bin/who
$ type cd
cd is a shell builtin
```

It is helpful to know what the shell provides versus what Linux does. The next few sections describe features of the shell.

Selected Features of the bash Shell

A shell does much more than simply run commands. It also has powerful features to make this task easier: wildcards for matching filenames, a "command history" to recall previous commands quickly, pipes for making the output of one command become the input of another, variables for storing values for use by the shell, and more. Take the time to learn these features, and you will become faster and more productive with Linux. Let's skim the surface and introduce you to these useful tools. (For full documentation, run info bash.)

Wildcards

Wildcards are a shorthand for sets of files with similar names. For example, a* means all files whose names begin with lowercase "a". Wildcards are "expanded" by the shell into the actual set of filenames they match. So if you type:

```
$ ls a*
```

the shell first expands a* into the filenames that begin with "a" in your current directory, as if you had typed:

```
$ ls aardvark adamantium apple
```

ls never knows you used a wildcard: it sees only the final list of filenames after the shell expands the wildcard. Importantly, this means *every* Linux command, regardless of its origin, works with wildcards and other shell features.

Wildcards never match two characters: a leading period, and the directory slash (/). These must be given literally, as in .pro* to match *.profile*, or /etc/*conf to match all filenames ending in *conf* in the */etc* directory.

Dot Files

Filenames with a leading period, called *dot files*, are special in Linux. When you name a file beginning with a period, it will not be displayed by some programs:

- ls will omit the file from directory listings, unless you provide the -a option
- Shell wildcards do not match a leading period

Effectively, dot files are hidden unless you explicitly ask to see them. As a result, sometimes they are called "hidden files."

Wildcard	Meaning
*	Zero or more consecutive characters
?	Any single character
[set]	Any single character in the given *set*, most commonly a sequence of characters, like [aeiouAEIOU] for all vowels, or a range with a dash, like [A-Z] for all capital letters
[^set]	Any single character *not* in the given *set* (as in the earlier example)
[!set]	Same as ^

When using character sets, if you want to include a literal dash in the set, put it first or last. To include a literal closing square bracket in the set, put it first. To include a ^ or ! symbol literally, don't put it first.

Brace expansion

Similar to wildcards, expressions with curly braces also expand to become multiple arguments to a command. The comma-separated expression:

```
{X,YY,ZZZ}
```

expands first to X, then YY, and finally ZZZ within a command line, like this:

```
$ echo sand{X,YY,ZZZ}wich
sandXwich sandYYwich sandZZZwich
```

Braces work with any strings, unlike wildcards, which are limited to filenames. The preceding example works regardless of which files are in the current directory.

Shell variables

You can define variables and their values by assigning them:

```
$ MYVAR=3
```

To refer to a value, simply place a dollar sign in front of the variable name:

```
$ echo $MYVAR
3
```

Some variables are standard and commonly defined by your shell upon login.

Variable	Meaning
DISPLAY	The name of your X window display
HOME	Your home directory, such as /home/smith
LOGNAME	Your login name, such as smith
MAIL	Your incoming mailbox, such as /var/spool/mail/smith
OLDPWD	Your shell's previous directory, prior to the last cd command
PATH	Your shell search path: directories separated by colons
PWD	Your shell's current directory
SHELL	The path to your shell, e.g., /bin/bash

Variable	Meaning
TERM	The type of your terminal, e.g., xterm or vt100
USER	Your login name

To see a shell's variables, run:

```
$ printenv
```

The scope of the variable (i.e., which programs know about it) is, by default, the shell in which it's defined. To make a variable and its value available to other programs your shell invokes (i.e., subshells), use the **export** command:

```
$ export MYVAR
```

or the shorthand:

```
$ export MYVAR=3
```

Your variable is now called an *environment variable*, since it's available to other programs in your shell's "environment." So in the preceding example, the exported variable MYVAR is available to all programs run by that same shell (including shell scripts: see "Variables" on page 196).

To make a variable value available to a specific program just once, prepend *variable=value* to the command line:

```
$ printenv HOME
/home/smith
$ HOME=/home/sally printenv HOME
/home/sally
$ printenv HOME
/home/smith                     The original value is unaffected
```

Search path

Programs are scattered all over the Linux filesystem, in directories like */bin* and */usr/bin*. When you run a program via a shell command, how does the shell find it? The critical variable PATH tells the shell where to look. When you type any command:

```
$ who
```

the shell has to find the who program by searching through Linux directories. The shell consults the value of PATH, which is a sequence of directories separated by colons:

```
$ echo $PATH
/usr/local/bin:/bin:/usr/bin:/home/smith/bin
```

and looks for the who command in each of these directories. If it finds who (say, /usr/bin/who), it runs the command. Otherwise, it reports:

```
bash: who: command not found
```

To add directories to your shell's search path temporarily, modify its PATH variable. For example, to append /usr/sbin to your shell's search path:

```
$ PATH=$PATH:/usr/sbin
$ echo $PATH
/usr/local/bin:/bin:/usr/bin:/home/smith/bin:/usr/sbin
```

This change affects only the current shell. To make it permanent, modify the PATH variable in your startup file ~/.bash_profile, as explained in "Tailoring Shell Behavior" on page 36. Then log out and log back in.

Aliases

The built-in command **alias** defines a convenient shorthand for a longer command, to save typing. For example:

```
$ alias ll='ls -l'
```

defines a new command ll that runs ls -l:

```
$ ll
total 436
-rw-r--r--    1 smith    3584 Oct 11 14:59 file1
-rwxr-xr-x    1 smith      72 Aug  6 23:04 file2
...
```

Define aliases in your ~/.bashrc file (see "Tailoring Shell Behavior" on page 36) to be available whenever you log in.[6] To list all your aliases, type **alias**. If aliases don't seem powerful

---

6. Some setups use a separate file, ~/.bash_aliases, for this purpose.

enough for you (since they have no parameters or branching), see "Programming with Shell Scripts" on page 195, run `info bash`, and read up on "shell functions."

Input/output redirection

The shell can redirect standard input, standard output, and standard error to and from files. In other words, any command that reads from standard input can have its input come from a file instead with the shell's < operator:

```
$ mycommand < infile
```

Likewise, any command that writes to standard output can write to a file instead:

```
$ mycommand > outfile          Create/overwrite outfile
$ mycommand >> outfile         Append to outfile
```

A command that writes to standard error can have its output redirected to a file as well, while standard output still goes to the screen:

```
$ mycommand 2> errorfile
```

To redirect both standard output and standard error to files:

```
$ mycommand > outfile 2> errorfile    Separate files
$ mycommand >& outfile                Single file
```

Pipes

You can redirect the standard output of one command to be the standard input of another, using the shell's pipe (|) operator. For example:

```
$ who | sort
```

sends the output of who into the sort program, printing an alphabetically sorted list of logged-in users. Multiple pipes work too. Here we sort the output of who again, extract the first column of information (using awk), and display the results one page at a time (using less):

```
$ who | sort | awk '{print $1}' | less
```

Combining commands

To invoke several commands in sequence on a single command line, separate them with semicolons:

```
$ command1 ; command2 ; command3
```

To run a sequence of commands as before, but stop execution if any of them fails, separate them with && ("and") symbols:

```
$ command1 && command2 && command3
```

To run a sequence of commands, stopping execution as soon as one succeeds, separate them with || ("or") symbols:

```
$ command1 || command2 || command3
```

Quoting

Normally, the shell treats whitespace simply as separating the words on the command line. If you want a word to *contain* whitespace (e.g., a filename with a space in it), surround it with single or double quotes to make the shell treat it as a unit. Single quotes treat their contents literally, while double quotes let shell constructs be evaluated, such as variables:

```
$ echo 'The variable HOME has value $HOME'
The variable HOME has value $HOME
$ echo "The variable HOME has value $HOME"
The variable HOME has value /home/smith
```

Backquotes ("backticks") cause their contents to be evaluated as a shell command. The contents are then replaced by the standard output of the command:

```
$ whoami            Program that prints your username
smith
$ echo My name is `whoami`
My name is smith
```

Escaping

If a character has special meaning to the shell but you want it used literally (e.g., * as a literal asterisk rather than a wildcard), precede the character with the backward slash "\" character. This is called *escaping* the special character:

```
$ echo a*                              As a wildcard, matching "a" filenames
aardvark  agnostic  apple
$ echo a\*                             As a literal asterisk
a*
$ echo "I live in $HOME"               Dollar sign means a variable value
I live in /home/smith
$ echo "I live in \$HOME"              A literal dollar sign
I live in $HOME
```

You can also escape control characters (tabs, newlines, ^D, and so forth) to have them used literally on the command line, if you precede them with ^V. This is particularly useful for tab (^I) characters, which the shell would otherwise use for filename completion (see "Filename completion" on page 31).

```
$ echo "There is a tab between here^V^I and here"
There is a tab between here        and here
```

Command-line editing

Bash lets you edit the command line you're working on, using keystrokes inspired by the text editors emacs and vi (see "File Creation and Editing" on page 54). To enable command-line editing with emacs keys, run this command (and place it in your *~/.bash_profile* to make it permanent):

```
$ set -o emacs
```

For vi keys:

```
$ set -o vi
```

emacs keystroke	vi keystroke (after ESC)	Meaning
^P or up arrow	k	Go to previous command
^N or down arrow	j	Go to next command
^F or right arrow	l	Go forward one character
^B or left arrow	h	Go backward one character
^A	0	Go to beginning of line
^E	$	Go to end of line
^D	x	Delete next character
^U	^U	Erase entire line

Command history

You can recall previous commands you've run—that is, the shell's *history*—and re-execute them. Some useful history-related commands are listed below.

Command	Meaning
history	Print your history
history *N*	Print the most recent *N* commands in your history
history -c	Clear (delete) your history
!!	Re-run previous command
!*N*	Re-run command number *N* in your history
!-*N*	Re-run the command you typed *N* commands ago
!$	Represents the last parameter from the previous command; great for checking that files are present before removing them:

```
$ ls a*
acorn.txt    affidavit
$ rm !$
```

!*	Represents all parameters from the previous command:

```
$ ls a b c
a    b    c
$ wc !*
    103    252   2904 a
     12     25    384 b
  25473  65510 988215 c
  25588  65787 991503 total
```

Filename completion

Press the TAB key while you are in the middle of typing a filename, and the shell will automatically complete (finish typing) the filename for you. If several filenames match what you've typed so far, the shell will beep, indicating the match is ambiguous. Immediately press TAB again and the shell will present the alternatives. Try this:

```
$ cd /usr/bin
$ ls un<TAB><TAB>
```

The shell will display all files in */usr/bin* that begin with *un*, such as *uniq*, *units*, and *unzip*. Type a few more characters to disambiguate your choice and press TAB again.

Shell Job Control

jobs	List your jobs.
&	Run a job in the background.
^Z	Suspend the current (foreground) job.
suspend	Suspend a shell.
fg	Unsuspend a job: bring it into the foreground.
bg	Make a suspended job run in the background.

All Linux shells have *job control*: the ability to run programs in the background (multitasking behind the scenes) and foreground (running as the active process at your shell prompt). A *job* is simply the shell's unit of work. When you run a command interactively, your current shell tracks it as a job. When the command completes, the associated job disappears. Jobs are at a higher level than Linux processes; the Linux operating system knows nothing about them. They are merely constructs of the shell. Some important vocabulary about job control is:

Foreground job
> Running in a shell, occupying the shell prompt so you cannot run another command

Background job
> Running in a shell, but not occupying the shell prompt, so you can run another command in the same shell

Suspend
> To stop a foreground job temporarily

Resume
> To cause a suspended job to start running again

jobs

The built-in command jobs lists the jobs running in your current shell.

```
$ jobs
[1]-  Running                 emacs myfile &
[2]+  Stopped                 su
```

The integer on the left is the job number, and the plus sign identifies the default job affected by the fg (foreground) and bg (background) commands.

&

Placed at the end of a command line, the ampersand causes the given command to run as a background job.

```
$ emacs myfile &
[2] 28090
```

The shell's response includes the job number (2) and the process ID of the command (28090).

^Z

Typing ^Z in a shell, while a job is running in the foreground, will suspend that job. It simply stops running, but its state is remembered.

```
$ mybigprogram
^Z
[1]+  Stopped                 mybigprogram
$
```

Now you're ready to type bg to put the command into the background, or fg to resume it in the foreground.

suspend

The built-in command suspend will suspend the current shell if possible, as if you'd typed ^Z to the shell itself. For instance, if you've run the su command and want to return to your original shell:

```
$ whoami
smith
$ su -l
Password: *******
# whoami
root
# suspend
[1]+  Stopped                 su
$ whoami
smith
```

---

bg

bg [%jobnumber]

The built-in command bg sends a suspended job to run in the background. With no arguments, bg operates on the most recently suspended job. To specify a particular job (shown by the jobs command), supply the job number preceded by a percent sign:

    $ bg %2

Some types of interactive jobs cannot remain in the background—for instance, if they are waiting for input. If you try, the shell will suspend the job and display:

    [2]+ Stopped   *command line here*

You can now resume the job (with fg) and continue.

---

fg

fg [%jobnumber]

The built-in command fg brings a suspended or backgrounded job into the foreground. With no arguments, it selects a job, usually the most recently suspended or backgrounded one. To specify a particular job (as shown by the jobs command), supply the job number preceded by a percent sign:

    $ fg %2

Killing a Command in Progress

If you've launched a command from the shell running in the foreground, and want to kill it immediately, type ^C. The shell recognizes ^C as meaning, "terminate the current foreground command right now." So if you are displaying a very long file (say, with the **cat** command) and want to stop, type ^C:

```
$ cat bigfile
This is a very long file with many lines. Blah blah blah
blah blah blah blahblahblah ^C
$
```

To kill a program running in the background, you can bring it into the foreground with **fg** and then type ^C, or alternatively, use the **kill** command (see "Controlling Processes" on page 121).

Typing ^C is not a friendly way to end a program. If the program has its own way to exit, use that when possible: see the sidebar for details.

Surviving a Kill

Killing a foreground program with ^C may leave your shell in an odd or unresponsive state, perhaps not displaying the keystrokes you type. This happens because the killed program had no opportunity to clean up after itself. If this happens to you:

1. Press ^J to get a shell prompt. This produces the same character as the Enter key (a newline) but will work even if Enter does not.

2. Type the shell command **reset** (even if the letters don't appear while you type) and press ^J again to run this command. This should bring your shell back to normal.

---

^C works only with shells. It will likely have no effect if typed in a window that is not a shell window. Additionally, some programs are written to "catch" the ^C and ignore it: an example is the text editor emacs.

Terminating a Shell

To terminate a shell, either run the **exit** command or type ^D.[7]

```
$ exit
```

Tailoring Shell Behavior

To configure all your shells to work in a particular way, edit the files *.bash_profile* and *.bashrc* in your home directory. These files execute each time you log in (*~/.bash_profile*) or open a shell (*~/.bashrc*). They can set variables and aliases, run programs, print your horoscope, or whatever you like.

These two files are examples of *shell scripts*: executable files that contain shell commands. We'll cover this feature in more detail in "Programming with Shell Scripts" on page 195.

This concludes our basic overview of Linux and the shell. Now we turn to Linux commands, listing and describing the most useful commands for working with files, processes, users, networking, multimedia, and more.

Basic File Operations

ls   List files in a directory.

cp   Copy a file.

mv   Rename ("move") a file.

rm   Delete ("remove") a file.

ln   Create links (alternative names) to a file.

One of the first things you'll need to do on a Linux system is manipulate files: copying, renaming, deleting, and so forth.

---

7. Control-D sends an "end of file" signal to any program reading from standard input. In this case, the program is the shell itself, which terminates.

`ls [options] [files]`

The ls command (pronounced as it is spelled, *ell ess*) lists attributes of files and directories. You can list files in the current directory:

```
$ ls
```

in given directories:

```
$ ls dir1 dir2 dir3
```

or individually:

```
$ ls file1 file2 file3
```

The most important options are -a, -l, and -d. By default, ls hides files whose names begin with a dot, as explained in the sidebar "Dot Files" on page 24. The -a option displays all files.

```
$ ls
myfile1    myfile2
$ ls -a
.hidden_file    myfile1    myfile2
```

The -l option produces a long listing:

```
-rw-r--r--    1 smith users        149 Oct 28  2011 my.data
```

that includes, from left to right: the file's permissions (-rw-r--r--), owner (smith), group (users), size (149 bytes), last modification date (Oct 28 2011) and name. See "File Protections" on page 20 for more information on permissions.

The -d option lists information about a directory itself, rather than descending into the directory to list its files.

```
$ ls -ld my.dir
drwxr-xr-x    1 smith users       4096 Oct 29  2011 my.dir
```

Useful options

- -a   List all files, including those whose names begin with a dot.

- -l   Long listing, including file attributes. Add the -h option (human-readable) to print file sizes in kilobytes, megabytes, and gigabytes, instead of bytes.

- -F   Decorate certain filenames with meaningful symbols, indicating their types. Appends "/" to directories, "*" to executables, "@" to symbolic links, "|" to named pipes, and "=" to sockets. These are just visual indicators for you, not part of the filenames!

-i Prepend the inode numbers of the files.

-s Prepend the size of the file in blocks, useful for sorting files by their size:

```
$ ls -s | sort -n
```

-R If listing a directory, list its contents recursively.

-d If listing a directory, do not list its contents, just the directory itself.

---

cp   stdin   stdout   - file   -- opt   --help   --version

cp [options] files (file | directory)

The cp command normally copies a file:

```
$ cp file file2
```

or copies multiple files into a directory:

```
$ cp file1 file2 file3 file4 destination_directory
```

Using the -a option, you can also recursively copy directories.

Useful options

-p Copy not only the file contents, but also the file's permissions, timestamps and, if you have sufficient permission to do so, its owner and group. (Normally the copies will be owned by you, timestamped now, with permissions set by applying your umask to the original permissions.)

-a Copy a directory hierarchy recursively, preserving all file attributes and links.

-r Copy a directory hierarchy recursively. This option does not preserve the files' attributes such as permissions and timestamps. It does preserve symbolic links.

-i Interactive mode. Ask before overwriting destination files.

-f Force the copy. If a destination file exists, overwrite it unconditionally.

---

mv   stdin   stdout   - file   -- opt   --help   --version

mv [options] source target

The mv (move) command can rename a file:

```
$ mv file1 file2
```

or move files and directories into a destination directory:

```
$ mv file1 file2 dir3 dir4 destination_directory
```

Useful options

- -i   Interactive mode. Ask before overwriting destination files.

- -f   Force the move. If a destination file exists, overwrite it unconditionally.

---

rm   stdin   stdout   - file   **- opt**   **--help**   **--version**

rm [*options*] *files | directories*

The rm (remove) command can delete files:

```
$ rm file1 file2 file3
```

or recursively delete directories:

```
$ rm -r dir1 dir2
```

Useful options

- -i   Interactive mode. Ask before deleting each file.

- -f   Force the deletion, ignoring any errors or warnings.

- -r   Recursively remove a directory and its contents. Use with caution, especially if combined with the - f option, as it can wipe out all your files.

---

ln   stdin   stdout   - file   **- opt**   **--help**   **--version**

ln [*options*] *source target*

A *link* is a reference to another file, created by the ln command. Intuitively, links give the same file multiple names, allowing it to live in two (or more) locations at once.

There are two kinds of links. A *symbolic link* (also called a *symlink* or *soft link*) refers to another file by its path, much like a Windows "shortcut" or a Macintosh "alias." To create a symbolic link, use the -s option:

```
$ ln -s myfile mysoftlink
```

If you delete the original file, the now-dangling link will be invalid, pointing to a nonexistent file path. A *hard link*, on the other hand, is simply a *second name* for a physical file on disk (in tech talk, it points to the same *inode*). If you delete the original file, the link still works. Figure 5 illustrates the difference. To create a hard link, type:

```
$ ln myfile myhardlink
```

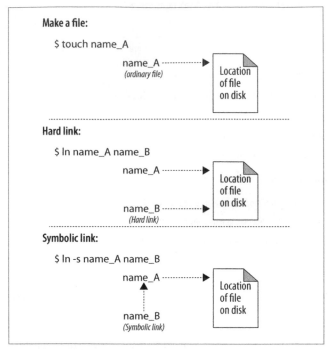

Figure 5. Hard link versus symbolic link

Symbolic links can point to files on other disk partitions, since they are just references to file paths; hard links cannot, since an inode on one disk has no meaning on another. Symbolic links can also point to directories, whereas hard links cannot...unless you are the superuser and use the -d option.

Useful options

- `-s`   Make a symbolic link. The default is a hard link.
- `-i`   Interactive mode. Ask before overwriting destination files.
- `-f`   Force the link. If a destination file exists, overwrite it unconditionally.
- `-d`   Create a hard link to a directory (superusers only).

It's easy to find out where a symbolic link points with either of these commands:

```
$ readlink linkname
$ ls -l linkname
```

Directory Operations

`cd`	Change your current directory.
`pwd`	Print the name of your current directory, i.e., "where you are now" in the filesystem.
`basename`	Print the final part of a file path.
`dirname`	Print a file path without its final part.
`mkdir`	Create (make) a directory.
`rmdir`	Delete (remove) an empty directory.
`rm -r`	Delete a nonempty directory and its contents.

We discussed the directory structure of Linux in "The Filesystem" on page 13. Now we'll cover commands that create, modify, delete, and manipulate directories within that structure.

---

cd   stdin   stdout   - file   -- opt   --help   --version

`cd [directory]`

The `cd` (change directory) command sets your current working directory:

```
$ cd /usr/games
```

With no directory supplied, cd defaults to your home directory:

```
$ cd
```

---

pwd   stdin **stdout** - file -- opt --help --version

pwd

The pwd command prints the absolute path of your current working directory:

```
$ pwd
/users/smith/mydir
```

---

basename   stdin **stdout** - file -- opt **--help** **--version**

basename *path* [*suffix*]

The basename command prints the final component in a file path:

```
$ basename /users/smith/finances/money.txt
money.txt
```

If you provide an optional suffix, it gets stripped from the result:

```
$ basename /users/smith/finances/money.txt .txt
money
```

---

dirname   stdin **stdout** - file -- opt **--help** **--version**

dirname *path*

The dirname command prints a file path with its final component removed:

```
$ dirname /users/smith/mydir
/users/smith
```

dirname does not change your current working directory. It simply manipulates a string, just like basename does.

mkdir

stdin   stdout   - file   -- opt   --help   --version

mkdir [*options*] *directories*

mkdir creates one or more directories:

    $ mkdir directory1 directory2 directory3

Useful options

-p	Given a directory path (not just a simple directory name), create any necessary parent directories automatically: mkdir -p /one/two/three creates */one* and */one/two* if they don't already exist, then */one/two/three*.
-m *mode*	Create the directory with the given permissions:

    $ mkdir -m 0755 mydir

By default, your shell's umask controls the permissions. See the chmod command in "File Properties" on page 59, and "File Protections" on page 20.

---

rmdir

stdin   stdout   - file   -- opt   --help   --version

rmdir [*options*] *directories*

The rmdir (remove directory) command deletes one or more empty directories you name:

    $ rmdir /tmp/junk

Useful options

-p If you supply a directory path (not just a simple directory name), delete not only the given directory, but the specified parent directories automatically, all of which must be empty. So rmdir -p /one/two/three will delete not only */one/ two/three*, but also */one/two* and */one*.

To delete a nonempty directory and its contents, use (carefully) rm -r *directory*. Use rm -ri to delete interactively, or rm -rf to annihilate without any error messages or confirmation.

File Viewing

`cat`	View files in their entirety.
`less`	View text files one page at a time.
`head`	View the first lines of a text file.
`tail`	View the last lines of a text file.
`nl`	View text files with their lines numbered.
`strings`	Display text that's embedded in a binary file.
`od`	View data in octal (or other formats).
`xxd`	View data in hexadecimal.
`acroread`	View PDF files.
`gv`	View PostScript or PDF files.
`xdvi`	View TeX DVI files.

In Linux, you'll encounter various types of files to view: plain text, PostScript, binary data, and more. Here we'll explain how to view them. Note that commands for viewing graphics files are covered in "Graphics and Screensavers" on page 181, and video files in "Video" on page 188.

---

cat   stdin   stdout   - file   -- opt   --help   --version

`cat [options] [files]`

The simplest viewer is `cat`, which just prints its files to standard output, concatenating them (hence the name). Large files will likely scroll off screen, so consider using `less` if you plan to read the output. That being said, `cat` is particularly useful for sending a set of files into a shell pipeline:

```
$ cat * | wc
```

`cat` can also manipulate its output in small ways, optionally displaying nonprinting characters, prepending line numbers (though `nl` is more powerful for this purpose), and eliminating whitespace.

Useful options

-T   Print tabs as ^I.

-E   Print newlines as $.

-v   Print other nonprinting characters in a human-readable format.

-n   Prepend line numbers to every line.

-b   Prepend line numbers to nonblank lines.

-s   Squeeze each sequence of blank lines into a single blank line.

---

less   stdin   stdout[8]   - file   -- opt   --help   --version

```
less [options] [files]
```

Use less to view text one "page" at a time (i.e., one window or screenful at a time). It's great for text files, or as the final command in a shell pipeline with lengthy output.

```
$ command1 | command2 | command3 | command4 | less
```

While running less, type h for a help message describing all its features. Here are some useful keystrokes for paging through files.

Keystroke	Meaning
h, H	View a help page.
Space bar, f, ^V, ^F	Move forward one screenful.
Enter	Move forward one line.
b, ^B, ESC-v	Move backward one screenful.
/	Enter search mode. Follow it with a regular expression and press Enter, and less will look for the first line matching it.
?	Same as /, but it searches backward in the file.
n	Repeat your most recent search forward.
N	Repeat your most recent search backward.

---

8. Although technically less can be plugged into the middle of a pipeline, or its output redirected to a file, there isn't much point to doing this.

Keystroke	Meaning
v	Edit the current file with your default text editor (the value of environment variable VISUAL, or if not defined, EDITOR, or if not defined, vi).
<	Jump to beginning of file.
>	Jump to end of file.
:n	Jump to next file.
:p	Jump to previous file.

less has a mind-boggling number of features; we're presenting only the most common. (For instance, less will display the contents of a compressed Zip file: try less myfile.zip.) The manpage is recommended reading.

Useful options

-c   Clear the screen before displaying the next page. This avoids scrolling and may be more comfortable on the eyes.

-m   Print a more verbose prompt, displaying the percentage of the file displayed so far.

-N   Display line numbers.

-r   Display control characters literally; normally less converts them to a human-readable format.

-s   Squeeze multiple, adjacent blank lines into a single blank line.

-S   Truncate long lines to the width of the screen, instead of wrapping.

---

head   stdin   stdout   - file   -- opt   --help   --version

head [*options*] [*files*]

The head command prints the first 10 lines of a file: great for previewing the contents.

```
$ head myfile
$ head * | less                     Preview all files in the current directory
```

It's also good for previewing the first few lines of output from a pipeline:

```
$ grep 'E' very-big-file | head
```

Useful options

-*N*   Print the first *N* lines instead of 10.

-n *N*   Print the first *N* lines instead of 10.

-c *N*   Print the first *N* bytes of the file.

-q   Quiet mode: when processing more than one file, don't print a banner above each file. Normally, head prints a banner containing the filename.

---

tail	stdin	stdout	- file	-- opt	--help	--version

```
tail [options] [files]
```

The **tail** command prints the last 10 lines of a file, and does other tricks as well.

```
$ tail myfile
```

The ultra-useful -f option causes **tail** to watch a file actively while another program is writing to it, displaying new lines as they are written to the file. This is invaluable for watching log files in active use:

```
$ tail -f /var/log/messages
```

Useful options

-*N*   Print the last *N* lines of the file instead of 10.

-n *N*   Print the last *N* lines of the file instead of 10.

-n +*N*   Print all lines except the first *N*.

-c *N*   Print the last *N* bytes of the file.

-f   Keep the file open, and whenever lines are appended to the file, print them. This is extremely useful. Add the --retry option if the file doesn't exist yet, but you want to wait for it to exist.

-q   Quiet mode: when processing more than one file, don't print a banner above each file. Normally tail prints a banner containing the filename.

---

nl [*options*] [*files*]

nl copies its files to standard output, prepending line numbers.

```
$ nl myfile
    1  Once upon a time, there was
    2  a little operating system named
    3  Linux, which everybody loved.
```

It's more flexible than cat with its -n and -b options, providing an
almost bizarre amount of control over the numbering. nl can be
used in two ways: on ordinary text files, and on specially marked-
up text files with predefined headers and footers.

Useful options

-b [a|t|n|p*R*]	Prepend numbers to all lines (a), nonblank lines (t), no lines (n), or only lines that contain regular expression *R*. (Default=a)
-v *N*	Begin numbering with integer *N*. (Default=1)
-i *N*	Increment the number by *N* for each line, so for example, you could use odd numbers only (-i2) or even numbers only (-v2 -i2). (Default=1)
-n [ln|rn|rz]	Format numbers as left-justified (ln), right-justified (rn), or right-justified with leading zeroes (rz). (Default=ln)
-w *N*	Force the width of the number to be *N* columns. (Default=6)
-s *S*	Insert string *S* between the line number and the text. (Default=TAB)

Additionally, nl has the wacky ability to divide text files into virtual
pages, each with a header, body, and footer with different numbering schemes. For this to work, however, you must insert nl-specific
delimiter strings into the file, such as \:\:\: (start of header),
\:\: (start of body), and \: (start of footer). Each must appear on
a line by itself. Then you can use additional options (see the manpage) to affect line numbering in the headers and footers of your
decorated file.

strings
stdin   stdout   - file   -- opt   --help   --version

strings [*options*] [*files*]

Binary files, such as executable programs and object files, usually contain some readable text. The strings program extracts that text and displays it on standard output. You can discover version information, authors' names, and other useful tidbits with strings.

```
$ strings /usr/bin/who
David MacKenzie
Copyright %s %d Free Software Foundation, Inc.
Report %s bugs to %s
...
```

Combine strings and grep to make your exploring more efficient. Here we look for email addresses:

```
$ strings /usr/bin/who | grep '@'
bug-coreutils@gnu.org
```

Useful options

-n *length*   Display only strings with length greater than *length* (the default is 4).

---

od
stdin   stdout   - file   -- opt   --help   --version

od [*options*] [*files*]

When you want to view a binary file, consider od (Octal Dump) for the job. It copies one or more files to standard output, displaying their data in ASCII, octal, decimal, hexadecimal, or floating point, in various sizes (byte, short, long). For example, this command:

```
$ od -w8 /usr/bin/who
0000000 042577 043114 000401 000001
0000010 000000 000000 000000 000000
0000020 000002 000003 000001 000000
...
```

displays the bytes in binary file */usr/bin/who* in octal, eight bytes per line. The column on the left contains the file offset of each row, again in octal.

If your binary file also contains text, consider the -tc option, which displays character data. For example, binary executables like who contain the string "ELF" at the beginning:

```
$ od -tc -w8 /usr/bin/who | head -3
0000000 177   E   L   F 001 001 001  \0
0000010  \0  \0  \0  \0  \0  \0  \0  \0
0000020 002  \0 003  \0 001  \0  \0  \0
```

Useful options

-N B	Display only the first B bytes of each file, specified in decimal, hexadecimal (by prepending 0x or 0X), 512-byte blocks (by appending b), kilobytes (by appending k), or megabytes (by appending m). (Default displays the entire file.)
-j B	Begin the output at byte B +1 of each file; acceptable formats are the same as for the -N option. (Default=0)
-w [B]	Display B bytes per line; acceptable formats are the same as in the -N option. Using -w by itself is equivalent to -w32. (Default=16)
-s [B]	Group each row of bytes into sequences of B bytes, separated by whitespace; acceptable formats are the same as in the -N option. Using -s by itself is equivalent to -s3. (Default=2)
-A (d|o|x|n)	Display file offsets in the leftmost column, in decimal (d), octal (o), hexadecimal (h), or not at all (n). (Default=o)
-t (a|c)[z]	Display output in a character format, with nonalphanumeric characters printed as escape sequences (c) or by name (a). For z, see below.
-t (d|o|u|x) [SIZE[z]]	Display output in an integer format, including octal (o), signed decimal (d), unsigned decimal (u), hexadecimal (x). (For binary output, use xxd instead.) SIZE represents the number of bytes per integer; it can be a positive integer or any of the values C, S, I, or L, which stand for the size of a char, short, int, or long datatype, respectively. For z, see below.
-t f[SIZE[z]]	Display output in floating point. SIZE represents the number of bytes per integer; it can be a positive integer or any of the values F, D, or L, which stand for the size of a float, double, or long double datatype, respectively. For z, see below. If -t is omitted, the default is -to2.

Appending z to the -t option prints a new column on the right-hand side of the output, displaying the printable characters on each line, much like the default output of xxd.

---

xxd

```
xxd [options] [files]
```

Similar to od, xxd produces a hexadecimal or binary dump of a file in several different formats. It can also do the reverse, converting from its hex dump format back into the original data. For example, here's a hex dump of binary file /usr/bin/who:

```
$ xxd /usr/bin/who
0000000: 7f45 4c46 0101 0100 0000 ... 0000  .ELF............
0000010: 0200 0300 0100 0000 a08c ... 0000  ............4...
0000020: 6824 0000 0000 0000 3400 ... 2800  h$......4. ...(.
0000030: 1900 1800 0600 0000 3400 ... 0408  ........4...4...
...
```

The left column indicates the file offset of the row, the next eight columns contain the data, and the final column displays the printable characters in the row, if any.

By default, xxd outputs three columns: file offsets, the data in hex, and the data as text (printable characters only).

Useful options

-l *N*	Display only the first *N* bytes. (Default displays the entire file,)
-s *N*	Skip the first *N* bytes of the file.
-s -*N*	Begin *N* bytes from the end of the file. (There is also a +*N* syntax for more advanced skipping through standard input; see the manpage.)
-c *N*	Display *N* bytes per row. (Default=16)
-g *N*	Group each row of bytes into sequences of *N* bytes, separated by whitespace, like od -s. (Default=2)
-b	Display the output in binary instead of hexadecimal.
-u	Display the output in uppercase hexadecimal instead of lowercase.
-p	Display the output as a plain hexdump, 60 contiguous bytes per line.

	The reverse operation: convert from an xxd hex dump back into the original file format. Works with the default hexdump format and, if you add the -p option, the plain hexdump format. If you're bored, try either of these commands to convert and unconvert a file in a pipeline, reproducing the original file on standard output:
-r	

```
$ xxd myfile | xxd -r
$ xxd -p myfile | xxd -r -p
```

-i	Display the output as a C programming language data structure. When reading from a file, it produces an array of unsigned chars containing the data, and an unsigned int containing the array length. When reading from standard input, it produces only a comma-separated list of hex bytes.

---

acroread

stdin   stdout   - file   -- opt   --help   --version

```
acroread [options] file.pdf
```

acroread is the official PDF reader from Adobe. It's easy to use and similar to Adobe Reader on Windows. You can also view PDF files with xpdf (*http://www.foolabs.com/xpdf/*) and gv.

---

gv

stdin   stdout   - file   -- opt   --help   --version

```
gv [options] file
```

GhostView displays an Adobe PostScript or PDF file in an X window. You can invoke it as gv or ghostview. Its basic operation is simple: click the desired page number to jump to that page, and so forth. A few minutes of playing around and you'll have the hang of it.

Useful options

-page *P*	Begin on page *P*. (Default=1)
-monochrome	Display in black and white.
-grayscale	Display in grayscale.
-color	Display in color.
-portrait	Choose portrait orientation.
-landscape	Choose landscape orientation.

-seascape	Choose upside-down landscape orientation.
-upsidedown	Choose upside-down portrait orientation.
-scale N	Zoom in or out. The integer N may be positive (make the image larger) or negative (smaller).
-watch	Automatically reload the PostScript file when it changes.
-nowatch	Do not automatically reload the PostScript file when it changes.

xdvi

stdin   stdout   - file   -- opt   --help   --version

xdvi [*options*] *file*

The document processing system TeX produces binary output files in a format called DVI, with suffix *.dvi*. The viewer xdvi displays a DVI file in an X window. While displaying a file, xdvi has a column of buttons down the right-hand side with obvious uses, such as Next to move to the next page. (You can hide the buttons by invoking xdvi with the -expert option.) You can also navigate the file by keystroke.

Keystroke	Meaning
q	Quit.
n	Jump to next page. (Alternatively, press Space bar, Enter, or Pagedown.) Precede it with a number N to jump by N pages.
p	Jump to previous page. (Alternatively, press Backspace, Delete, or Pageup.) Precede it with a number N to jump by N pages.
<	Jump to first page.
>	Jump to last page.
^L	Redisplay the page.
R	Reread the DVI file, say, after you've modified it.
Any mouse button	Magnify a rectangular region under the mouse cursor.

xdvi has dozens of command-line options for tailoring its colors, geometry, zoom, and overall behavior.

If you prefer, convert a DVI file to PostScript via the dvips command and then use GhostView (gv) to display it:

```
$ dvips -o myfile.ps myfile.dvi
$ gv myfile.ps
```

File Creation and Editing

Command	Meaning
emacs	Text editor from Free Software Foundation.
vim	Text editor, extension of Unix vi.
soffice	Office suite for editing Microsoft Word, Excel, and PowerPoint documents.
abiword	Edit Microsoft Word documents.
gnumeric	Edit Excel spreadsheets.

To get far with Linux, you must become proficient with one of its text editors. The two major ones are emacs from the Free Software Foundation, and vim, a successor to the Unix editor vi. Teaching these editors fully is beyond the scope of this book, but both have online tutorials, and we list common operations in Table 1. To edit a file, run either:

```
$ emacs myfile
$ vim myfile
```

If *myfile* doesn't exist, it is created automatically.

In case you share files with Microsoft Windows systems, we will also cover Linux programs that edit Microsoft Word, Excel, and PowerPoint documents.

Creating a File Quickly

You can quickly create an empty file (for later editing) using the touch command:

```
$ touch newfile
```

or the `echo -n` command (see "File Properties" on page 59):[9]

```
$ echo -n > newfile2
```

or write data into a new file by redirecting the output of a program (see "Input/output redirection" on page 28):

```
$ echo anything at all > newfile
```

Your Default Editor

Various Linux programs will run an editor when necessary, and by default the editor is vim. For example, your email program may invoke an editor to compose a new message, and `less` invokes an editor if you type "v". But what if you don't want vim to be your default editor? Set the environment variables VISUAL and EDITOR to your choice, for example:

```
$ EDITOR=emacs
$ VISUAL=emacs
$ export EDITOR VISUAL          Optional
```

Both variables are necessary because different programs check one variable or the other. Set EDITOR and VISUAL in your ~/.bash_profile startup file if you want your choices made permanent. Any program can be made your default editor as long as it accepts a filename as an argument.

Regardless of how you set these variables, all system administrators should know at least basic vim and emacs commands in case a system tool suddenly runs an editor on a critical file.

---

emacs   stdin   stdout   - file   -- opt   --help   --version

```
emacs [options] [files]
```

emacs is an extremely powerful editing environment with more commands than you could possibly imagine, plus a complete

---

9. The -n option prevents a newline character from being written to the file, making it truly empty.

programming language to define your own editing features. To invoke emacs in a new X window, run:

```
$ emacs
```

To run in a existing shell window:

```
$ emacs -nw
```

Now to invoke the built-in emacs tutorial, type ^h t.

Most emacs keystroke commands involve the control key (like ^F) or the *meta* key, which is usually the Escape key or the Alt key. emacs's own documentation notates the meta key as M- (as in M-F to mean "hold the meta key and type F"), so we will too. For basic keystrokes, see Table 1.

---

vim   stdin   stdout   - file   -- opt   --help   --version

```
vim [options] [files]
```

vim is an enhanced version of the old standard Unix editor vi. To invoke the editor in a new X window, run:

```
$ gvim
```

To run in a existing shell window:

```
$ vim
```

To run the vim tutorial, run:

```
$ vimtutor
```

vim is a mode-based editor. It operates in two modes, *insert* and *normal*. Insert mode is for entering text in the usual manner, while normal mode is for running commands like "delete a line" or copy/paste. For basic keystrokes in normal mode, see Table 1.

Table 1. Basic keystrokes in emacs and vim

Task	emacs	vim
Type text	Just type	Type i, then any text, and finally ESC
Save and quit	^x^s then ^x^c	:wq
Quit without saving	^x^c Respond "no" when asked to save buffers	:q!
Save	^x^s	:w
Save As	^x^w	:w *filename*
Undo	^/ or ^x u	u
Suspend editor (not in X)	^z	^z
Switch to edit mode	*(N/A)*	ESC
Switch to command mode	M-x	:
Abort command in progress	^g	ESC
Move forward	^f or right arrow	l or right arrow
Move backward	^b or left arrow	h or left arrow
Move up	^p or up arrow	k or up arrow
Move down	^n or down arrow	j or down arrow
Move to next word	M-f	w
Move to previous word	M-b	b
Move to beginning of line	^a	0
Move to end of line	^e	$
Move down one screen	^v	^f
Move up one screen	M-v	^b
Move to beginning of buffer	M-<	gg
Move to end of buffer	M->	G
Delete next character	^d	x
Delete previous character	BACKSPACE	X

Task	emacs	vim
Delete next word	M-d	de
Delete previous word	M-BACKSPACE	db
Delete current line	^a^k	dd
Delete to end of line	^k	d$
Define region (type this keystroke to mark the beginning of the region, then move the cursor to the end of the desired region)	^ Space bar	v
Cut region	^w	d
Copy region	M-w	y
Paste region	^y	p
Get help	^h	:help
View the manual	^h i	:help

---

soffice

stdin   stdout   - file   -- opt   --help   --version

soffice [*files*]

OpenOffice.org[10] is a comprehensive, integrated office software suite that can edit Microsoft Word, Excel, and PowerPoint files. Simply run:

    $ soffice

and you're ready to work. The same program edits all three types of files.[11] It is a large program that requires plenty of memory and disk space.

OpenOffice.org can also handle drawings (oodraw command), databases (oobase), and mathematical formulas (oomath).

---

10. The ".org" is part of the software package's name.

11. Under the hood, soffice comprises the separate programs Writer (oowriter command) for word processing, Calc (oocalc) for spreadsheets, and Impress (ooimpress) for presentations, which you can run directly if desired.

OpenOffice.org has more information, or you can use the soffice Help menu.

Some distros supply a different package, LibreOffice, a spin-off of OpenOffice.org with the same commands. See *http://www.libreoffice.org/* for details.

---

abiword   stdin   stdout   - file   -- opt   **--help**   **--version**

abiword [*options*] [*files*]

abiword is another program for editing Microsoft Word documents. It is smaller and quicker than soffice, though not as powerful, and perfectly suitable for many editing tasks.

    $ abiword myfile.doc

If you specify files on the command line, they must exist: abiword won't create them for you.

---

gnumeric   stdin   stdout   - file   -- opt   **--help**   **--version**

gnumeric [*options*] [*files*]

gnumeric is a spreadsheet program that can edit Microsoft Excel documents. It is quite powerful and fast, and if you've used Excel before, gnumeric will feel familiar.

    $ gnumeric myfile.xls

If you specify files on the command line, they must exist: gnumeric won't create them for you.

File Properties

stat	Display attributes of files and directories.
wc	Count bytes, words, lines in a file.
du	Measure disk usage of files and directories.
file	Identify (guess) the type of a file.
touch	Change timestamps of files and directories.

chown	Change owner of files and directories.
chgrp	Change group ownership of files and directories.
chmod	Change protection mode of files and directories.
umask	Set a default mode for new files and directories.
chattr	Change extended attributes of files and directories.
lsattr	List extended attributes of files and directories.

When examining a Linux file, keep in mind that the contents are only half the story. Every file and directory also has attributes that describe its owner, size, access permissions, and other information. The ls -l command (see "Basic File Operations" on page 36) displays some of these attributes, but other commands provide additional information.

---

stat

stdin   **stdout**   - file   **-- opt**   **--help**   **--version**

stat [*options*] *files*

The stat command lists important attributes of files (by default) or filesystems (-f option). File information looks like:

```
$ stat myfile
  File: "myfile"
  Size: 1264        Blocks: 8         Regular File
  Access: (0644/-rw-r--r--) Uid: (600/lisa) Gid: (620/users)
  Device: 30a       Inode: 99492      Links: 1
  Access: Fri Aug 29 00:16:12 2003
  Modify: Wed Jul 23 23:09:41 2003
  Change: Wed Jul 23 23:11:48 2003
```

and includes the filename, size in bytes (1264), size in blocks (8), file type (Regular File), permissions in octal (0644), permissions in the format of "ls -l" (-rw-r--r--), owner's user ID (600), owner's name (lisa), owner's group ID (620), owner's group name (users), device type (30a), inode number (99492), number of hard links (1), and timestamps of the file's most recent access, modification, and status change. Filesystem information looks like:

```
$ stat -f myfile
  File: "myfile"
```

```
      ID: bffff358 ffffffff Namelen: 255    Type: EXT2
 Blocks: Total: 2016068    Free: 876122    Available:
 773709      Size: 4096
 Inodes: Total: 1026144    Free: 912372
```

and includes the filename (*myfile*), filesystem ID (bffff358 ffffffff), maximum length of a filename for that filesystem (255 bytes), filesystem type (EXT2), the counts of total, free, and available blocks in the filesystem (2016068, 876122, and 773709, respectively), block size for the filesystem (4096), and the counts of total and free inodes (1026144 and 912372, respectively).

The -t option presents the same data but on a single line, without headings. This is handy for processing by shell scripts or other programs:

```
$ stat -t myfile
myfile 1264 8 81a4 500 500 30a 99492 1 44 1e 1062130572
  1059016181 1059016308
$ stat -tf myfile
myfile bffff358 ffffffff 255 ef53 2016068 875984 773571
  4096 1026144 912372
```

Useful options

- -L   Follow symbolic links and report on the file they point to.

- -f   Report on the filesystem containing the file, not the file itself.

- -t   Terse mode: print information on a single line.

WC

stdin stdout - file -- opt --help --version

wc [*options*] [*files*]

The wc (word count) program prints a count of bytes, words, and lines in (presumably) a text file.

```
$ wc myfile
  24      62     428 myfile
```

This file has 24 lines, 62 whitespace-delimited words, and 428 bytes.

Useful options

-l   Print the line count only.

-w   Print the word count only.

-c   Print the byte count only.

-L   Locate the longest line in each file and print its length in bytes.

---

du   stdin   **stdout**   - file   -- **opt**   --**help**   --**version**

```
du [options] [files| directories]
```

The du (disk usage) command measures the disk space occupied by files or directories. By default, it measures the current directory and all its subdirectories, printing totals in blocks for each, with a grand total at the bottom.

```
$ du
8      ./Notes
36     ./Mail
340    ./Files/mine
40     ./Files/bob
416    ./Files
216    ./PC
2404 .
```

It can also measure the size of files:

```
$ du myfile myfile2
4      myfile
16     myfile2
```

Useful options

-b   Measure usage in bytes.

-k   Measure usage in kilobytes.

-m   Measure usage in megabytes.

-B *N*   Display sizes in blocks that you define, where 1 block = *N* bytes. (Default = 1024)

-h -H   Print in human-readable units. For example, if two directories are of size 1 gigabyte or 25 kilobytes, respectively, du -h prints 1G and 25K. The -h option uses powers of 1024, whereas -H uses powers of 1000.

`-c`	Print a total in the last line. This is the default behavior when measuring a directory, but for measuring individual files, provide `-c` if you want a total.
`-L`	Follow symbolic links and measure the files they point to.
`-s`	Print only the total size.

file

file [*options*] *files*

The file command reports the type of a file:

```
$ file /etc/hosts /usr/bin/who letter.doc
/etc/hosts:      ASCII text
/usr/bin/who:    ELF 32-bit LSB executable, Intel 80386 ...
letter.doc:      Microsoft Office Document
```

Unlike some other operating systems, Linux does not keep track of file types, so the output is an educated guess based on the file content and other factors.

Useful options

`-b`	Omit filenames (left column of output).
`-i`	Print MIME types for the file, such as "text/plain" or "audio/mpeg", instead of the usual output.
`-f` *name_file*	Read filenames, one per line, from the given *name_file*, and report their types. Afterward, process filenames on the command line as usual.
`-L`	Follow symbolic links, reporting the type of the destination file instead of the link.
`-z`	If a file is compressed (see "File Compression and Packaging" on page 92), examine the uncompressed contents to decide the file type, instead of reporting "compressed data."

touch

touch [*options*] *files*

The touch command changes two timestamps associated with a file: its modification time (when the file's data was last changed) and its access time (when the file was last read). To set both timestamps to right now, run:

```
$ touch myfile
```

You can set these timestamps to arbitrary values, e.g.:

```
$ touch -d "November 18 1975" myfile
```

If a given file doesn't exist, touch creates it, a handy way to create empty files.

Useful options

-a	Change the access time only.
-m	Change the modification time only.
-c	If the file doesn't exist, don't create it (normally, touch creates it).
-d *timestamp*	Set the file's timestamp(s). A tremendous number of timestamp formats are acceptable, from "12/28/2001 3pm" to "28-May" (the current year is assumed, and a time of midnight) to "next tuesday 13:59" to "0" (midnight today). Experiment and check your work with stat. Full documentation is available from info touch.
-t *timestamp*	A less intelligent way to set the file's *timestamp*, using the format [[*CC*]*YY*]*MMDDhhmm*[.*ss*], where *CC* is the two-digit century, *YY* is the two-digit year, *MM* is the 2-digit month, *DD* is the two-digit day, *hh* is the two-digit hour, *mm* is the two-digit minute, and *ss* is the two-digit second. For example, -t 20030812150047 represents August 12, 2003, at 15:00:47.

---

chown
stdin   stdout   - file   **-- opt**   **--help**   **--version**

chown [*options*] *user_spec files*

The chown (change owner) command sets the ownership of files and directories. To make user smith the owner of several files and a directory, run:

```
# chown smith myfile myfile2 mydir
```

The *user_spec* parameter may be any of these possibilities:

- A username (or numeric user ID), to set the owner: chown smith myfile

---

- A username (or numeric user ID), optionally followed by a colon and a group name (or numeric group ID), to set the owner and group: `chown smith:users myfile`
- A username (or numeric user ID) followed by a colon, to set the owner *and* to set the group to the invoking user's login group: `chown smith: myfile`
- A group name (or numeric group ID) preceded by a colon, to set the group only: `chown :users myfile`
- `--reference=`*file* to set the same owner and group as another given file

Useful options

`--dereference`	Follow symbolic links and operate on the files they point to.
`-R`	Recursively change the ownership within a directory hierarchy.

---

chgrp

stdin   stdout   - file   **-- opt**   **--help**   **--version**

`chgrp [`*options*`] `*group_spec files*

The `chgrp` (change group) command sets the group ownership of files and directories.

```
$ chgrp smith myfile myfile2 mydir
```

The *group_spec* parameter may be any of these possibilities:

- A group name or numeric group ID
- `--reference=`*file*, to set the same group ownership as another given file

See "Group Management" on page 140 for more information on groups.

Useful options

`--dereference`	Follow symbolic links and operate on the files they point to.
`-R`	Recursively change the ownership within a directory hierarchy.

chmod [*options*] *permissions files*

The chmod (change mode) command protects files and directories from unauthorized users on the same system, by setting access permissions. Typical permissions are read, write, and execute, and they may be limited to the file owner, the file's group owner, and/or other users. The permissions argument can take three different forms:

- --reference= *file*, to set the same permissions as another given file.

- An octal number, up to four digits long, that specifies the file's *absolute* permissions in bits, as in Figure 6. The leftmost digit is special (described later) and the second, third, and fourth represent the file's owner, the file's group, and all users.

- One or more strings specifying *absolute or relative* permissions (i.e., relative to the file's existing permissions). For example, a+r makes a file readable by all users.

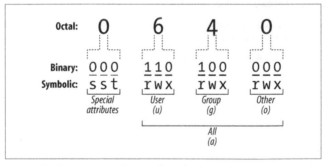

Figure 6. File permission bits explained

In the third form, each string consists of three parts: an optional *scope*, a *command*, and *permissions*.

Scope (optional)
> u for user, g for group, o for other users not in the group, a for all users. The default is a.

Command

> \+ to add permissions; - to remove permissions; or = to set absolute permissions, ignoring existing ones.

Permissions

> r for read, w for write/modify, x for execute (for directories, this is permission to cd into the directory), X for conditional execute (explained later), u to duplicate the user permissions, g to duplicate the group permissions, o to duplicate the "other users" permissions, s for setuid or setgid, and t for the sticky bit.

For example, ug+rw would add read and write permission for the user and the group, a-x (or just -x) would remove execute permission for everyone, and u=r would first remove all existing permissions and then make the file readable only by its owner. You can combine these strings by separating them with commas, such as ug+rw,a-x.

Conditional execute permission (X) means the same as x, except that it succeeds only if the file is already executable, or if the file is a directory. Otherwise, it has no effect.

Setuid and setgid apply to executable files (programs and scripts). Suppose we have an executable file *F* owned by user "smith" and the group "friends". If file *F* has setuid (set user ID) enabled, then anyone who runs *F* will "become" user smith, with all her rights and privileges, for the duration of the program. Likewise, if *F* has setgid (set group ID) enabled, anyone who executes *F* becomes a member of the friends group for the duration of the program. As you might imagine, setuid and setgid can impact system security, so don't use them unless you *really* know what you're doing. One misplaced chmod +s can leave your whole system vulnerable to attack.

The sticky bit, most commonly used for */tmp* directories, controls removal of files in that directory. Normally, if you have write permission in a directory, you can delete or move files within it, even if you don't have this access to the files themselves. Inside a directory with the sticky bit set, you need write permission on a file in order to delete or move it.

Useful options

-R   Recursively change the ownership within a directory hierarchy.

---

umask   stdin **stdout** - file -- opt --help --version

umask [*options*] [*mask*]

The umask command sets or displays your default mode for creating
files and directories: whether they are readable, writable, and/or
executable by yourself, your group, and the world.

```
$ umask
0002
$ umask -S
u=rwx,g=rwx,o=rx
```

Let's start with some technical talk and follow with common-sense
advice. A umask is a binary (base two) value, though it is commonly
presented in octal (base eight). It defines your default protection
mode by combining with the octal value 0666 for files and 0777 for
directories, using the binary operation NOT AND. For example, the
umask 0002 yields a default file mode of 0664:

```
0666 NOT AND 0002
= 000110110110 NOT AND 000000000010
= 000110110110 AND 111111111101
= 000110110100
= 0664
```

Similarly for directories, 0002 NOT AND 0777 yields a default mode of
0775.

If that explanation seems from outer space, here are some simple
recipes. Use mask 0022 to give yourself full privileges, and all others
read/execute privileges only:

```
$ umask 0022
$ touch newfile && mkdir dir
$ ls -ld newfile dir
-rw-r--r--    1 smith smith         0 Nov 11 12:25 newfile
drwxr-xr-x    2 smith smith      4096 Nov 11 12:25 dir
```

Use mask 0002 to give yourself and your default group full privileges, and read/execute to others:

```
$ umask 0002
$ touch newfile && mkdir dir
$ ls -ld newfile dir
-rw-rw-r--    1 smith smith         0 Nov 11 12:26 newfile
drwxrwxr-x    2 smith smith      4096 Nov 11 12:26 dir
```

Use mask 0077 to give yourself full privileges with nothing for anyone else:

```
$ umask 0077
$ touch newfile && mkdir dir
$ ls -ld newfile dir
-rw-------    1 smith smith         0 Nov 11 12:27 newfile
drwx------    2 smith smith      4096 Nov 11 12:27 dir
```

---

chattr

stdin   stdout   - file   -- opt   --help   --version

chattr [options] [+ - =]attributes [files]

If you grew up with other Unix systems, you might be surprised that Linux files can have additional attributes beyond their access permissions. If a file is on an "ext" filesystem (ext2, ext3, etc.), you can set these extended attributes with the chattr (change attribute) command and list them with lsattr.

As with chmod, attributes may be added (+) or removed (-) relatively, or set absolutely (=). For example, to keep a file compressed and nondumpable, run:

```
$ chattr +cd myfile
```

Attribute	Meaning
a	Append-only: appends are permitted to this file, but it cannot otherwise be edited. Root only.
A	Accesses not timestamped: accesses to this file don't update its access timestamp (atime).
c	Compressed: data is transparently compressed on writes and uncompressed on reads.
d	Don't dump: tell the dump program to ignore this file when making backups (see "Backups and Remote Storage" on page 111).
i	Immutable: file cannot be changed or deleted (root only).
j	Journaled data (ext3 filesystems only).

Attribute	Meaning
s	Secure deletion: if deleted, this file's data is overwritten with zeroes.
S	Synchronous update: changes are written to disk immediately, as if you had typed sync after saving (see "Disks and Filesystems" on page 106).
u	Undeletable: file cannot be deleted.

There are a few other attributes too, some of them obscure or experimental. See the manpage for details.

Useful options

-R   Recursively process directories.

---

lsattr   stdin   **stdout**   - file   **-- opt**   **--help**   --version

lsattr [*options*] [*files*]

If you set extended attributes with chattr, you can view them with lsattr (list attributes). The output uses the same letters as chattr; for example, this file is immutable and undeletable:

```
$ lsattr myfile
-u--i--- myfile
```

With no files specified, lsattr prints the attributes of all files in the current directory.

Useful options

-R   Recursively process directories.

-a   List all files, including those whose names begin with a dot.

-d   If listing a directory, do not list its contents, just the directory itself.

File Location

find	Locate files in a directory hierarchy.
xargs	Process a list of located files (and much more).
locate	Create an index of files, and search the index for string.

---

which	Locate executables in your search path (command).
type	Locate executables in your search path (bash built-in).
whereis	Locate executables, documentation, and source files.

Linux systems can contain hundreds of thousands of files easily. How can you find a particular file when you need to? The first step is to organize your files logically into directories in some thoughtful manner, but there are several other ways to find files, depending on what you're looking for.

For finding any file, **find** is a brute-force program that slogs file-by-file through a directory hierarchy to locate a target. **locate** is much faster, searching through a prebuilt index that you generate as needed. (Some distros generate the index nightly by default.)

For finding programs, the **which** and **type** commands check all directories in your shell search path. **type** is built into the bash shell (and therefore available only when you're running bash), while **which** is a program (normally */usr/bin/which*); **type** is faster and can detect shell aliases.[12] In contrast, **whereis** examines a known set of directories, rather than your search path.

---

find   stdin   **stdout**   - file   -- opt   **--help**   **--version**

`find [directories] [expression]`

The **find** command searches one or more directories (and their subdirectories recursively) for files matching certain criteria. It is very powerful, with over 50 options and, unfortunately, a rather unusual syntax. Here are some simple examples that search the entire filesystem from the root directory:

Find a particular file named *myfile*:

```
$ find / -type f -name myfile -print
```

---

12. The **tcsh** shell performs some trickery to make **which** detect aliases.

Print all directory names:

```
$ find / -type d -print
```

Print filenames ending in ".txt" (notice how the wildcard is escaped so the shell ignores it):

```
$ find / -type f -name \*.txt -print
```

Useful options

-name *pattern* -path *pattern* -lname *pattern*	The name (-name), pathname (-path), or symbolic link target (-lname) of the desired file must match this shell pattern, which may include shell wildcards *, ?, and []. (You must escape the wildcards, however, so they are ignored by the shell and passed literally to find.) Paths are relative to the directory tree being searched.
-iname *pattern* -ipath *pattern* -ilname *pattern*	The -iname, -ipath and -ilname options are the same as -name, -path, and -lname, respectively, but are case-insensitive.
-regex *regexp*	The path (relative to the directory tree being searched) must match the given regular expression.
-type *t*	Locate only files of type *t*. This includes plain files (f), directories (d), symbolic links (l), block devices (b), character devices (c), named pipes (p), and sockets (s).
-atime *N* -ctime *N* -mtime *N*	File was last accessed (-atime), last modified (-mtime), or had a status change (-ctime) exactly *N**24 hours ago. Use +*N* for "greater than *N*," or -*N* for "less than *N*."
-amin *N* -cmin *N* -mmin *N*	File was last accessed (-amin), last modified (-mmin), or had a status change (-cmin) exactly *N* minutes ago. Use +*N* for "greater than *N*," or -*N* for "less than *N*."
-anewer *other_file* -cnewer *other_file* -newer *other_file*	File was accessed (-anewer), modified (-newer), or had a status change (-cnewer) more recently than *other_file* has.
-maxdepth *N* -mindepth *N*	Consider files at least (-mindepth) or at most (-maxdepth) *N* levels deep in the directory tree being searched.

-follow	Dereference symbolic links.
-depth	Proceed using depth-first search: completely search a directory's contents (recursively) before operating on the directory itself.
-xdev	Limit the search to a single filesystem, i.e., don't cross device boundaries.
-size N [bckw]	Consider files of size N, which can be given in blocks (b), one-byte characters (c), kilobytes (k), or two-byte words (w). Use +N for "greater than N," or -N for "less than N."
-empty	File has zero size, and is a regular file or directory.
-user name	File is owned by the given user.
-group name	File is owned by the given group.
-perm mode	File has permissions equal to mode. Use - mode to check that *all* of the given bits are set, or +mode to check that *any* of the given bits are set.

You can group and negate parts of the expression with the following operators:

expression1 -a *expression2*
> And. (This is the default if two expressions appear side by side, so the "-a" is optional.)

expression1 -o *expression2*
> Or.

! *expression*
-not *expression*
> Negate the expression.

(*expression*)
> Precedence markers, just like in algebra class. Evaluate what's in parentheses first. You may need to escape these from the shell with "\".

expression1 , *expression2*
> Same as the comma operator in the C programming language. Evaluate both expressions and return the value of the second one.

Once you've specified the search criteria, you can tell find to perform these actions on files that match the criteria.

Useful options

-print	Simply print the path to the file, relative to the search directory.
-printf *string*	Print the given string, which may have substitutions applied to it in the manner of the C library function, printf( ). See the manpage for the full list of outputs.
-print0	Like -print, but instead of separating each line of output with a newline character, use a null (ASCII 0) character. Use when piping the output of find to another program, and your list of filenames may contain space characters. Of course, the receiving program must be capable of reading and parsing these null-separated lines—for example, xargs -0.
-exec *cmd* ;	Invoke the given shell command, *cmd*. Make sure to escape any shell metacharacters, including the required, final semicolon, so they are not immediately evaluated on the command line. Also, the symbol "{}" (make sure to quote or escape it) represents the path to the file found.
-ok *cmd* ;	Same as -exec, but also prompts the user before invoking each command.
-ls	Perform the command ls -dils on the file.

---

xargs   stdin   stdout   -file   --opt   **--help**   **--version**

xargs [*options*] [*command*]

xargs is one of the oddest yet most powerful commands available to the shell. It reads lines of text from standard input, turns them into commands, and executes them. This might not sound exciting, but xargs has some unique uses, particularly for processing a list of files you've located. Suppose you made a file named *important* that lists important files, one per line:

```
$ cat important
/home/jsmith/mail/love-letters
/usr/local/lib/critical_stuff
```

```
/etc/passwd
...
```

With `xargs`, you can process each of these files easily with other
Linux commands. For instance, the following command runs the
`ls -l` command on all the listed files:

```
$ cat important | xargs ls -l
```

Similarly, you can view the files with `less`:

```
$ cat important | xargs less
```

and even delete them with `rm`:

```
$ cat important | xargs rm -f
```

Each of these pipelines reads the list of files from *important* and
produces and runs new Linux commands based on the list. The
power begins when the input list doesn't come from a file, but from
another command writing to standard output. In particular, the
`find` command, which prints a list of files on standard output,
makes a great partner for `xargs`. For example, to search your current
directory hierarchy for files containing the word "myxomatosis":

```
$ find . -print | xargs grep -l myxomatosis
```

This power comes with one warning: if any of the files located by
`find` contains whitespace in its name, this will confuse `grep`. If one
file is named (say) *my stuff*, then the `grep` command constructed is:

```
$ grep -l myxomatosis my stuff
```

which tells `grep` to process *two* files named *my* and *stuff*. Oops! Now
imagine if the program had been `rm` instead of `grep`. You'd be telling
`rm` to delete the wrong files! To avoid this problem, always use `find`
`-print0` instead of `-print`, which separates lines with ASCII null
characters instead of newline characters, combined with `xargs -0`,
which expects ASCII nulls:

```
$ find . -print0 | xargs -0 grep -l myxomatosis
```

We have barely scratched the surface of the `xargs` command, so
please experiment! (With harmless commands like `grep` and `ls` at
first!)

Useful options

- -n *k* Feed *k* lines of input to the command being executed. A common scenario is to use -n1, guaranteeing that each execution will process only one line of input. Otherwise, xargs may pass multiple lines of input to a single command.

- -0 Set the end-of-line character for input to be ASCII zero rather than whitespace, and treat all characters literally. Use this when the input is coming from find -print0.

---

xargs Versus Backquotes

If you remember "Quoting" on page 29, you might realize that some xargs tricks can be accomplished with backquotes:

```
$ cat file_list | xargs rm -f     with xargs
$ rm -f `cat file_list`           with backquotes
```

While both commands do similar things, backquotes can fail if the command line gets so long, after the quoted part is expanded, that it exceeds the maximum length of a shell command line. xargs does not have this limitation, so it's safer and more suitable for large or risky operations.

---

locate   stdin   **stdout**   - file   -- opt   **--help**   **--version**

locate [*options*]

The locate command, with its partner updatedb, creates an index (database) of file locations that is quickly searchable.[13] If you plan to locate many files over time in a directory hierarchy that doesn't change much, locate is a good choice. For locating a single file or performing more complex processing of found files, use find.

Some distros automatically index the entire filesystem on a regular basis (e.g., once a day), so you can simply run locate and it will

---

13. Our locate command comes from a package called "mlocate." Some systems have an older package called "slocate" with slightly different usage. If you have slocate, simply type slocate instead of updatedb in our examples.

work. But if you ever need to create an index yourself of a directory and all its subdirectories (say, storing it in */tmp/myindex*), run:

```
$ updatedb -l0 -U directory -o /tmp/myindex
```

(Note that -l0 is a lowercase L followed by a zero, not the number 10.) Then to search for a string in the index:

```
$ locate -d /tmp/myindex string
```

locate has an interesting, optional security feature. You can create an index that, when searched, will display only files that the user is permitted to see. So if the superuser created an index of a protected directory, a non-superuser could search it but not see the protected files. This is done by omitting the -l0 option to updatedb and running it as root:

```
# updatedb -U directory -o /tmp/myindex
```

Indexing options for updatedb

-u	Create index from the root directory downward.
-U *directory*	Create index from *directory* downward.
-l (0|1)	Turn security off (0) or on (1). The default is 1.
-e *directories*	Exclude one or more directories from the index. Separate their paths by commas.
-o *outfile*	Write the index to file *outfile*.

Search options for locate

-d *index*	Indicate which index to use (in our example, */tmp/myindex*).
-i	Case-insensitive search.
-r *regexp*	Search for files matching the given regular expression.

---

which   stdin   **stdout**   - file   **-- opt**   **--help**   **--version**

which *file*

The which command locates an executable file in your shell's search path. If you've been invoking a program by typing its name:

```
$ who
```

---

the which command tells you where this command is located:

```
$ which who
/usr/bin/who
```

You can even find the which program itself:

```
$ which which
/usr/bin/which
```

If several programs in your search path have the same name (for example, */usr/bin/who* and */usr/local/bin/who*), which reports only the first.

---

type   stdin **stdout** - file **-- opt** --help --version

type [*options*] *commands*

The type command, like which, locates an executable file in your shell's search path:

```
$ type grep who
grep is /bin/grep
who is /usr/bin/who
```

However, type is built into the bash shell, whereas which is a program on disk:

```
$ type which type rm if
which is /usr/bin/which
type is a shell builtin
rm is aliased to `/bin/rm -i'
if is a shell keyword
```

As a built-in command, type is faster than which; however, it's available only if you're running bash.

---

whereis   stdin **stdout** - file -- opt --help --version

whereis [*options*] *files*

The whereis command attempts to locate the given files by searching a hardcoded list of directories. It can find executables, documentation, and source code. whereis is somewhat quirky because its list of directories might not include the ones you need.

Useful options

-b	List only executables (-b), manpages (-m), or source code files (-s).
-m	
-s	
-B *dirs...* -f	Search for executables (-B), manpages (-M), or source code files
-M *dirs...* -f	(-S) only in the given directories. You must follow the directory list with the -f option before listing the files you seek.
-S *dirs...* -f	

File Text Manipulation

grep	Find lines in a file that match a regular expression.
cut	Extract columns from a file.
paste	Append columns.
tr	Translate characters into other characters.
sort	Sort lines of text by various criteria.
uniq	Locate identical lines in a file.
tee	Copy a file *and* print it on standard output, simultaneously.

Perhaps Linux's greatest strength is text manipulation: massaging a text file (or standard input) into a desired form by applying transformations, often in a pipeline. Any program that reads standard input and writes standard output falls into this category, but here we'll present some of the most important tools.

---

grep   stdin   stdout   - file   -- opt   --help   --version

grep [*options*] *pattern* [*files*]

The grep command is one of the most consistently useful and powerful in the Linux arsenal. Its premise is simple: given one or more files, print all lines in those files that match a particular regular expression pattern. For example, if a file contains these lines:

```
The quick brown fox jumped over the lazy dogs!
My very eager mother just served us nine pancakes.
Film at eleven.
```

and we search for all lines containing "pancake", we get:

```
$ grep pancake myfile
My very eager mother just served us nine pancakes.
```

Now we use a regular expression to match lines ending in an exclamation point:

```
$ grep '\!$' myfile
The quick brown fox jumped over the lazy dogs!
```

grep can use two different types of regular expressions, which it calls *basic* and *extended*. They are equally powerful, just different, and you may prefer one over the other based on your experience with other grep implementations. The basic syntax is in Table 2.

Useful options

-v	Print only lines that *do not* match the regular expression.
-l	Print only the *names* of files that contain matching lines, not the lines themselves.
-L	Print only the names of files that *do not* contain matching lines.
-c	Print only a count of matching lines.
-n	In front of each line of matching output, print its original line number.
-b	In front of each line of matching output, print the byte offset of the line in the input file.
-i	Case-insensitive match.
-w	Match only complete words (i.e., words that match the entire regular expression).
-x	Match only complete lines (i.e., lines that match the entire regular expression). Overrides -w.
-A N	After each matching line, print the next N lines from its file.
-B N	Before each matching line, print the previous N lines from its file.
-C N	Same as -A N -B N: print N lines (from the original file) above *and* below each matching line.

--color=always	Highlight the matched text in color, for better readability.
-r	Recursively search all files in a directory and its subdirectories.
-E	Use extended regular expressions. See egrep.
-F	Use lists of fixed strings instead of regular expressions. See fgrep.

---

egrep   stdin   stdout   - file   -- opt   --help   --version

egrep [*options*] *pattern* [*files*]

The egrep command is just like grep, but uses a different ("extended") language for regular expressions. It's the same as grep -E.

Table 2. Regular expressions for grep and egrep

Regular expression		
Plain	**Extended**	**Meaning**
.		Any single character.
[...]		Match any single character in this list.
[^...]		Match any single character NOT in this list.
(...)		Grouping.
|	|	Or.
^		Beginning of a line.
$		End of a line.
\<		Beginning of a word.
\>		End of a word.
[:alnum:]		Any alphanumeric character.
[:alpha:]		Any alphabetic character.
[:cntrl:]		Any control character.
[:digit:]		Any digit.
[:graph:]		Any graphic character.
[:lower:]		Any lowercase letter.
[:print:]		Any printable character.

Regular expression		
Plain	Extended	Meaning
[:punct:]		Any punctuation mark.
[:space:]		Any whitespace character.
[:upper:]		Any uppercase letter.
[:xdigit:]		Any hexadecimal digit.
*		Zero or more repetitions of a regular expression.
\+	+	One or more repetitions of a regular expression.
\?	?	Zero or one occurrence of a regular expression.
\{ n \}	{ n }	Exactly n repetitions of a regular expression.
\{ n ,\}	{ n ,}	n or more repetitions of a regular expression.
\{ n , m \}	{ n , m }	Between n and m (inclusive) repetitions of a regular expression, $n < m$.
\c		The character c literally, even if c is a special regular expression character. For example, use * to match an asterisk or \\ to match a backslash. Alternatively, put the literal character inside square brackets, like [*] or [\].

grep and End-of-Line Characters

When you match the end of a line ($) with grep, text files created on Microsoft Windows or Macintosh OS X systems may produce odd results. The reason is that each operating system has a different standard for ending a line. On Linux, each line in a text file ends with a newline character (ASCII 10). On Windows, text lines end with two characters: a carriage return (ASCII 13) followed by a newline character. And on Macintosh, a text file might end its lines with newlines or carriage returns alone. If grep isn't matching the ends of lines properly, check for non-Linux end-of-line characters with cat -v, which displays carriage returns as ^M:

```
$ cat -v dosfile
Uh-oh! This file seems to end its lines with^M
carriage returns before the newlines.^M
```

To remove the carriage returns, use the `tr -d` command:

```
$ tr -d '\r' < dosfile > newfile
$ cat -v newfile
Uh-oh! This file seems to end its lines with
carriage returns before the newlines.
```

fgrep

fgrep [*options*] [*fixed_strings*] [*files*]

The `fgrep` command is just like `grep`, but instead of accepting a regular expression, it accepts a list of fixed strings, separated by newlines. It's the same as `grep -F`. For example, if you have a dictionary file full of strings, one per line:

```
$ cat my_dictionary_file
aardvark
aback
abandon
...
```

you can conveniently search for those strings in a set of input files:

```
$ fgrep -f my_dictionary_file inputfile1 inputfile2
```

Normally, you'll use the lowercase `-f` option to make `fgrep` read the fixed strings from a file. You can also read the fixed strings on the command line using quoting, but it's a bit trickier. To search for the strings one, two, and three in a file, you'd type:

```
$ fgrep 'one            Note we are typing newline characters
two
three' myfile
```

`fgrep` is convenient when searching for nonalphanumeric characters like * and { because they are taken literally, not as regular expression characters.

cut   stdin   stdout   - file   -- opt   --help   --version

cut -(b|c|f)*range* [*options*] [*files*]

The cut command extracts columns of text from files. A "column" is defined by character offsets (e.g., the nineteenth character of each line):

    $ cut -c19 myfile

or by byte offsets (which are often the same as characters, unless you have multibyte characters in your language):

    $ cut -b19 myfile

or by delimited fields (e.g., the fifth field in each line of a comma-delimited file):

    $ cut -f5 -d, myfile

You aren't limited to printing a single column: you can provide a range (3-16), a comma-separated sequence (3,4,5,6,8,16), or both (3,4,8-16). For ranges, if you omit the first number (-16), a 1 is assumed (1-16); if you omit the last number (5-), the end of line is used.

Useful options

-d *C*	Use character *C* as the *input* delimiter character between fields for the - f option. By default it's a tab character.
--output-delimiter=*C*	Use character *C* as the *output* delimiter character between fields for - f. By default it's a tab character.
-s	Suppress (don't print) lines that don't contain the delimiter character.

---

paste   stdin   stdout   - file   -- opt   --help   --version

paste [*options*] [*files*]

The paste command is the opposite of cut: it treats several files as vertical columns and combines them on standard output:

    $ cat letters
    A

```
B
C
$ cat numbers
1
2
3
4
5
$ paste numbers letters
1   A
2   B
3   C
4
5
$ paste letters numbers
A   1
B   2
C   3
    4
    5
```

Useful options

-d *delimiters*	Use the given *delimiters* characters between columns; the default is a tab character. Provide a single character (-d:) to be used always, or a list of characters (-dxyz) to be applied in sequence on each line (the first delimiter is x, then y, then z, then x, then y, ...).
-s	Transpose the rows and columns of output:

```
$ paste -s letters numbers
A   B   C
1   2   3   4   5
```

---

tr   stdin   stdout   - file   -- opt   **--help**   **--version**

tr [*options*] *charset1* [*charset2*]

The tr command performs some simple, useful translations of one set of characters into another. For example, to capitalize everything in a file:

```
$ cat myfile
This is a very wonderful file.
```

```
$ cat myfile | tr 'a-z' 'A-Z'
THIS IS A VERY WONDERFUL FILE.
```

or to change all vowels into asterisks:

```
$ cat myfile | tr aeiouAEIOU '*'
Th*s *s * v*ry w*nd*rf*l f*l*.
```

or to delete all vowels:

```
$ cat myfile | tr -d aeiouAEIOU
Ths s  vry wndrfl fl.
```

As a very practical example, delete all carriage returns from a DOS text file so it's more compatible with Linux text utilities like grep:

```
$ tr -d '\r' < dosfile > newfile
```

tr translates the first character in *charset1* into the first character in *charset2*, the second into the second, the third into the third, etc. If the length of *charset1* is N, only the first N characters in *charset2* are used. (If *charset1* is longer than *charset2*, see the -t option.)

Character sets can have the following forms.

Form	Meaning
ABCD	The sequence of characters A, B, C, D.
A-B	The range of characters from A to B.
[x*y]	y repetitions of the character x.
[:*class*:]	The same character classes ([:alnum:], [:digit:], etc.) accepted by grep.

tr also understands the escape characters "\a" (^G = ring bell), "\b" (^H = backspace), "\f" (^L = formfeed), "\n" (^J = newline), "\r" (^M = return), "\t" (^I = tab), and "\v" (^K = vertical tab) accepted by printf (see "Screen Output" on page 168), as well as the notation \nnn to mean the character with octal value *nnn*.

tr is great for quick and simple translations, but for more powerful jobs consider sed, awk, or perl.

Useful options

-d   Delete the characters in *charset1* from the input.

-s   Eliminate adjacent duplicates (found in *charset1*) from the input. For example, `tr -s aeiouAEIOU` would squeeze adjacent, duplicate vowels to be single vowels (reeeeeeally would become really).

-c   Operate on all characters *not* found in *charset1*.

-t   If *charset1* is longer than *charset2*, make them the same length by truncating *charset1*. If -t is not present, the last character of *charset2* is (invisibly) repeated until *charset2* is the same length as *charset1*.

---

sort   stdin   stdout   - file   -- opt   --help   --version

```
sort [options] [files]
```

The sort command prints lines of text in alphabetical order, or sorted by some other rule you specify. All provided files are concatenated, and the result is sorted and printed.

```
$ cat myfile
def
xyz
abc
$ sort myfile
abc
def
xyz
```

Useful options

-f   Case-insensitive sorting.

-n   Sort numerically (i.e., 9 comes before 10) instead of alphabetically (10 comes before 9 because it begins with a "1").

-g   Another numerical sorting method with a different algorithm that, among other things, recognizes scientific notation (7.4e3 means "7.4 times ten to the third power," or 7400). Run `info sort` for full technical details.

-u   Unique sort: ignore duplicate lines. (If used with -c for checking sorted files, fail if any consecutive lines are identical.)

-c   Don't sort, just check if the input is already sorted. If it is, print nothing; otherwise, print an error message.

-b	Ignore leading whitespace in lines.
-r	Reverse the output: sort from greatest to least.
-t X	Use X as the field delimiter for the -k option.
-k key	Choose sorting keys. (Combine with -t to choose a separator character between keys.)

A sorting key is a portion of a line that's considered when sorting, instead of considering the entire line. An example is "the fifth character of each line." Normally, sort would consider these lines to be in sorted order:

```
aaaaz
bbbby
```

but if your sorting key is "the fifth character of each line," then the lines are reversed because y comes before z. A more practical example involves this file of names and addresses:

```
$ cat people
George Washington,123 Main Street,New York
Abraham Lincoln,54 First Avenue,San Francisco
John Adams,39 Tremont Street,Boston
```

An ordinary sort would display the "Abraham Lincoln" line first. But if you consider each line as three comma-separated values, you can sort on the second value with:

```
$ sort -k2 -t, people
George Washington,123 Main Street,New York
John Adams,39 Tremont Street,Boston
Abraham Lincoln,54 First Avenue,San Francisco
```

where "123 Main Street" is first alphabetically. Likewise, you can sort on the city (third value) with:

```
$ sort -k3 -t, people
John Adams,39 Tremont Street,Boston
George Washington,123 Main Street,New York
Abraham Lincoln,54 First Avenue,San Francisco
```

and see that Boston comes up first alphabetically. The general syntax -k $F1[.C1][,F2[.C2]]$ means:

Item	Meaning	Default if not supplied
F1	Starting field	Required
C1	Starting position within field 1	1
F2	Ending field	Last field
C2	Starting position within ending field	1

So `sort -k1.5` sorts based on the first field, beginning at its fifth character; and `sort -k2.8,5` means "from the eighth character of the second field, to the first character of the fifth field." The `-t` option changes the behavior of `-k` so it considers delimiter characters such as commas rather than spaces.

You can repeat the `-k` option to define multiple keys, which will be applied from first to last as found on the command line.

---

uniq

stdin   stdout   - file   -- opt   --help   --version

`uniq [options] [files]`

The `uniq` command operates on consecutive, duplicate lines of text. For example, if you have a file *myfile*:

```
$ cat myfile
a
b
b
c
b
```

then `uniq` would detect and process (in whatever way you specify) the two consecutive b's, but not the third b.

```
$ uniq myfile
a
b
c
b
```

uniq is often used after sorting a file:

```
$ sort myfile | uniq
a
b
c
```

In this case, only a single b remains because all three were made adjacent by sort, then collapsed to one by uniq. Also, you can count duplicate lines instead of eliminating them:

```
$ sort myfile | uniq -c
      1 a
      3 b
      1 c
```

Useful options

-c   Count adjacent duplicate lines.

-i   Case-insensitive operation.

-u   Print unique lines only.

-d   Print duplicate lines only.

-s *N*   Ignore the first *N* characters on each line when detecting duplicates.

-f *N*   Ignore the first *N* whitespace-separated fields on each line when detecting duplicates.

-w *N*   Consider only the first *N* characters on each line when detecting duplicates. If used with -s or -f, sort will ignore the specified number of characters or fields first, then consider the next *N* characters.

---

tee   stdin   stdout   - file   -- opt   --help   --version

tee [*options*] *files*

Like the cat command, the tee command copies standard input to standard output unaltered. Simultaneously, however, it also copies that same standard input to one or more files. tee is most often found in the middle of pipelines, writing some intermediate data to a file while also passing it to the next command in the pipeline:

```
$ who | tee original_who | sort
```

In this command line, tee writes the output of who to the file original_who, and then passes along that same output to the rest of the pipeline (sort), producing sorted output on screen.

Useful options

- -a   Append instead of overwriting files.
- -i   Ignore interrupt signals.

More Powerful Manipulations

We've just touched the tip of the iceberg for Linux text filtering. Linux has hundreds of filters that produce ever more complex manipulations of the data. But with great power comes a great learning curve, too much for a short book. Here are a few filters to get you started.

awk

awk is a pattern-matching language. It matches data by regular expression and then performs actions based on the data. Here are a few simple examples for processing a text file, *myfile*.

Print the second and fourth word on each line:

```
$ awk '{print $2, $4}' myfile
```

Print all lines that are shorter than 60 characters:

```
$ awk 'length < 60 {print}' myfile
```

sed

Like awk, sed is a pattern-matching engine that can perform manipulations on lines of text. Its syntax is closely related to that of vim and the line editor ed. Here are some trivial examples.

Print the file with all occurrences of the string "red" changed to "hat":

```
$ sed 's/red/hat/g' myfile
```

Print the file with the first 10 lines removed:

```
$ sed '1,10d' myfile
```

---

m4

m4 is a macro-processing language and command. It locates keywords within a file and substitutes values for them. For example, given this file:

```
$ cat myfile
My name is NAME and I am AGE years old
ifelse(QUOTE,yes,No matter where you go... there you are)
```

see what m4 does with substitutions for NAME, AGE, and QUOTE:

```
$ m4 -DNAME=Sandy myfile
My name is Sandy and I am AGE years old

$ m4 -DNAME=Sandy -DAGE=25 myfile
My name is Sandy and I am 25 years old

$ m4 -DNAME=Sandy -DAGE=25 -DQUOTE=yes myfile
My name is Sandy and I am 25 years old
No matter where you go... there you are
```

Perl, PHP, Python

Perl, PHP, and Python are full-fledged scripting languages powerful enough to build complete, robust applications. See "Beyond Shell Scripting" on page 208 for references.

File Compression and Packaging

tar	Package multiple files into a single file.
gzip	Compress files with GNU Zip.
gunzip	Uncompress GNU Zip files.
bzip2	Compress files in BZip format.
bunzip2	Uncompress BZip files.
bzcat	Compress/uncompress BZip files via standard input/output.
compress	Compress files with traditional Unix compression.
uncompress	Uncompress files with traditional Unix compression.
zcat	Compress/uncompress file via standard input/output (gzip or compress).
zip	Compress files in Windows Zip format.

unzip	Uncompress Windows Zip files.
metamail	Extract MIME data to files.

Linux can compress files into a variety of formats and uncompress them. The most popular formats are GNU Zip (**gzip**), whose compressed files are named with the *.gz* suffix, and BZip, which uses the *.bz2* suffix. Other common formats include Zip files from Windows systems (*.zip* suffix) and occasionally, classic Unix compression (*.Z* suffix).

A related technology involves converting binary files into textual formats, so they can (say) be transmitted within an email message. Nowadays this is done automatically with attachments and MIME tools, but we'll cover the **metamail** program, which can do this from the command line.

If you come across a format we don't cover, such as Macintosh sit files, Arc, Zoo, rar, and others, learn more at *http://en.wiki pedia.org/wiki/List_of_archive_formats*.

---

tar
stdin   stdout   - file   -- opt   --help   --version

```
tar [options] [files]
```

The tar program was originally for backing up files onto a tape drive (its name is short for "tape archive"). Although tape has lost its popularity, **tar** is still the most common file-packaging format for Linux. It can pack multiple files and directories into a single file for transport, optionally compressed.

```
$ tar -czvf myarchive.tar.gz mydir      Create
$ tar -tzvf myarchive.tar.gz            List contents
$ tar -xzvf myarchive.tar.gz            Extract
```

If you actually have a tape drive, simply specify the drive's device (such as */dev/tape*) as the destination file:

```
$ tar -cf /dev/tape myfile1 myfile2
```

If you specify files on the command line, only those files are processed:

```
$ tar -xvf myarchive.tar file1 file2 file3
```

Otherwise, the entire archive is processed.

Useful options

-c   Create an archive. You'll have to list the input files and directories on the command line.

-r   Append files to an existing archive.

-u   Append new/changed files to an existing archive.

-A   Append one archive to the end of another: e.g., `tar -A -f first.tar second.tar` appends the contents of *second.tar* to *first.tar*. Does not work for compressed archives.

-t   List the archive.

-x   Extract files from the archive.

-f *file* Read the archive from, or write the archive to, the given file. This is usually a tar file on disk (such as *myarchive.tar*) but can also be a tape drive (such as */dev/tape*).

-d   Diff (compare) the archive against the filesystem.

-z   Use gzip compression.

-j   Use bzip2 compression.

-Z   Use Unix compression.

-b *N*   Use a block size of *N* * 512 bytes.

-v   Verbose mode: print extra information.

-h   Follow symbolic links rather than merely copying them.

-p   When extracting files, restore their original permissions and ownership.

---

gzip   stdin   stdout - file -- opt --help --version

gzip [*options*] [*files*]

gzip and gunzip compress and uncompress files in GNU Zip format. Compressed files have the suffix *.gz*.

Sample commands

gzip *file*   Compress *file* to create *file.gz*. Original *file* is deleted.

`gzip -c file`	Produce compressed data on standard output.
`cat file | gzip`	Produce compressed data from a pipeline.
`gunzip file.gz`	Uncompress *file.gz* to create *file*. Original *file.gz* is deleted.
`gunzip -c file.gz`	Uncompress the data on standard output.
`cat file.gz | gunzip`	Uncompress the data from a pipeline.
`zcat file.gz`	Uncompress the data on standard output.

gzipped tar files: sample commands

`tar -czf myfile.tar.gz dirname`	Pack directory *dirname*.
`tar -tzf myfile.tar.gz`	List contents.
`tar -xzf myfile.tar.gz`	Unpack.

Add the -v option to tar to print filenames as they are processed.

---

bzip2   stdin   stdout   - file   -- opt   --help   --version

`bzip2 [options] [files]`

bzip2 and bunzip2 compress and uncompress files in Burrows-Wheeler format. Compressed files have the suffix *.bz2*.

Sample commands

`bzip2 file`	Compress *file* to create *file.bz2*. Original *file* is deleted.
`bzip2 -c file`	Produce compressed data on standard output.
`cat file | bzip2`	Produce compressed data on standard output.
`bunzip2 file.bz2`	Uncompress *file.bz2* to create *file*. Original *file.bz2* is deleted.
`bunzip2 -c file.bz2`	Uncompress the data on standard output.

| `cat file.bz2 \| bunzip2` | Uncompress the data on standard output. |
| `bzcat file.bz2` | Uncompress the data on standard output. |

bzipped tar files: sample commands

`tar -cjf myfile.tar.bz2 dirname`	Pack.
`tar -tjf -myfile.tar.bz2`	List contents.
`tar -xjf myfile.tar.bz2`	Unpack.

Add the -**v** option to **tar** to print filenames as they are processed.

---

compress   stdin   stdout   - file   -- opt   --help   --version

`compress [options] [files]`

compress and uncompress compress and uncompress files in standard Unix compression format (Lempel Ziv). Compressed files have the suffix .Z.

Sample commands

`compress file`	Compress file to create file.Z. Original file is deleted.
`compress -c file`	Produce compressed data on standard output.
`cat file | compress`	Produce compressed data from a pipeline.
`uncompress file.Z`	Uncompress file.Z to create file. Original file.Z is deleted.
`uncompress -c file.Z`	Uncompress the data on standard output.
`cat file.Z | uncompress`	Uncompress the data from a pipeline.
`zcat file.Z`	Uncompress the data on standard output.

Compressed tar files: sample commands

| `tar -cZf myfile.tar.Z dirname` | Pack directory dirname. |
| `tar -tZf myfile.tar.Z` | List contents. |

```
tar -xZf myfile.tar.Z          Unpack.
```

Add the -v option to tar to print filenames as they are processed.

---

zip   stdin   stdout   - file   -- opt   **--help**   **--version**

```
zip [options] [files]
```

zip and unzip compress and uncompress files in Windows Zip format. Compressed files have the suffix *.zip*. Unlike most other Linux compression commands, zip does not delete the original files.

```
zip myfile.zip file1 file2 file3 ...    Pack.
zip -r myfile.zip dirname               Pack recursively.
unzip -l myfile.zip                     List contents.
unzip myfile.zip                        Unpack.
```

---

metamail   stdin   stdout   - file   -- opt   --help   --version

```
metamail [options] mail_file
```

Modern email programs can send and receive attachments so easily we rarely think about it, but this was not always the case. Programs like metamail were created to work with attachments directly on the command line, appending or extracting them to and from mail messages. For example, if you have an email message in a file, *mymessage*, and it contains a JPEG image as an attachment, metamail can extract the image:

```
$ metamail -w mymessage
Content-Description: coolcat.jpg
This message contains 'image/jpeg`-format data.
Please enter the name of a file to which the data should
 be written (Default: coolcat.jpg) > hotdog.jpg
Wrote file hotdog.jpg
```

Here we extracted the attached JPEG file, *coolcat.jpg*, renaming it as *hotdog.jpg*. The -w option tells metamail to write the data to a file; otherwise, metamail would attempt to display the attachment with an appropriate program, such as an image viewer:

```
$ metamail mymessage
This message contains 'image/jpeg'-format data.
Do you want to view it using the 'xv' command (y/n) [y] y
---Executing: gthumb
```

File Comparison

diff	Line-by-line comparison of two files or directories.
comm	Line-by-line comparison of two sorted files.
cmp	Byte-by-byte comparison of two files.
md5sum	Compute a checksum of the given files (MD5).

There are three ways to compare Linux files:

- Line by line (diff, diff3, sdiff, comm), best suited to text files
- Byte by byte (cmp), often used for binary files
- By comparing checksums (md5sum, sum, cksum)

These programs are all text-based. For a graphical file-comparison tool, try **xxdiff** at *http://furius.ca/xxdiff*.

---

diff   stdin   **stdout**   - file   -- opt   **--help**   **--version**

```
diff [options] file1 file2
```

The diff command compares two files line-by-line, or two directories. When comparing text files, diff can produce detailed reports of their differences. For binary files, diff merely reports whether they differ or not. For all files, if there are no differences, diff produces no output.

The traditional output format looks like this:

> *Indication of line numbers and the type of change*
> < *Corresponding section of file1, if any*
> ---
> > *Corresponding section of file2, if any*

For example, if we start with a file *fileA*:

```
Hello, this is a wonderful file.
The quick brown fox jumped over
the lazy dogs.
Goodbye for now.
```

Suppose we delete the first line, change "brown" to "blue" on the second line, and add a final line, creating a file *fileB*:

```
The quick blue fox jumped over
the lazy dogs.
Goodbye for now.
Linux r00lz!
```

Then `diff fileA fileB` produces this output:

```
1,2c1                                       fileA lines 1-2 became fileB line 1
< Hello, this is a wonderful file.  Lines 1-2 of fileA
< The quick brown fox jumped over
---                                         diff separator
> The quick blue fox jumped over    Line 1 of fileB
4a4                                         Line 4 was added in fileB
> Linux r00lz!                              The added line
```

The leading symbols < and > are arrows indicating *fileA* and *fileB*, respectively. This output format is the default: many others are available, some of which can be fed directly to other tools. Try them out to see what they look like.

Option	Output format
-n	RCS version control format, as produced by `rcsdiff` (man `rcsdiff`).
-c	Context diff format, as used by the `patch` command (man `patch`).
-D *macro*	C preprocessor format, using `#ifdef` *macro* ... `#else` ... `#endif`.
-u	Unified format, which merges the files and prepends "-" for deletion and "+" for addition.
-y	Side-by-side format; use -W to adjust the width of the output.
-e	Create an ed script that would change *fileA* into *fileB* if run.
-q	Don't report changes, just say whether the files differ.

`diff` can also compare directories:

```
$ diff dir1 dir2
```

which compares any same-named files in those directories, and lists all files that appear in one directory but not the other. To compare entire directory hierarchies recursively, use the -r option:

```
$ diff -r dir1 dir2
```

which produces a (potentially massive) report of all differences.

Useful options

-b   Don't consider whitespace.

-B   Don't consider blank lines.

-i   Ignore case.

-r   When comparing directories, recurse into subdirectories.

diff is just one member of a family of programs that operate on file differences. Some others are diff3, which compares three files at a time, and sdiff, which merges the differences between two files to create a third file according to your instructions.

---

comm	stdin	**stdout**	- file	-- opt	--help	--version

comm [*options*] *file1* *file2*

The comm command compares two sorted files and produces three columns of output, separated by tabs:

1. All lines that appear in *file1* but not in *file2*.

2. All lines that appear in *file2* but not in *file1*.

3. All lines that appear in both files.

For example, if *file1* and *file2* contain these lines:

file1:	*file2:*
apple	baker
baker	charlie
charlie	dark

then comm produces this three-column output:

```
$ comm file1 file2
apple
                baker
                charlie
        dark
```

Useful options

-1   Suppress column 1.

-2   Suppress column 2.

-3   Suppress column 3.

---

cmp   stdin   stdout   - file   -- opt   --help   --version

cmp [*options*] *file1* *file2* [*offset1* [*offset2*]]

The cmp command compares two files. If their contents are the same, cmp reports nothing; otherwise, it lists the location of the first difference:

```
$ cmp myfile yourfile
myfile yourfile differ: char 494, line 17
```

By default, cmp does not tell you what the difference is, only where it is. It also is perfectly suitable for comparing binary files, as opposed to diff, which operates best on text files.

Normally, cmp starts its comparison at the beginning of each file, but it will start elsewhere if you provide offsets:

```
$ cmp myfile yourfile 10 20
```

This begins the comparison at the tenth character of *myfile* and the twentieth of *yourfile*.

Useful options

-l   Long output: print all differences, byte by byte:

```
$ cmp -l myfile yourfile
494 164 172
```

This means at offset 494 (in decimal), *myfile* has "t" (octal 164) but *yourfile* has "z" (octal 172).

-s   Silent output: don't print anything, just exit with an appropriate return code; 0 if
the files match, 1 if they don't. (Or other codes if the comparison fails for some
reason.)

---

md5sum   stdin   stdout   -file   --opt   --help   --version

md5sum *files* | --check *file*

The md5sum command works with checksums to verify that files are
unchanged. The first form produces the 32-byte checksum of the
given files, using the MD5 algorithm:

```
$ md5sum myfile
dd63602df1cceb57966d085524c3980f  myfile
```

while the second form tests whether a checksum matches its file,
using --check:

```
$ md5sum file1 file2 file3 > mysum
$ cat mysum
90a022707ca5b5fc8f465e7cbb954987  file1
86d19ef79d33c28cf0c9ba882f25cdb8  file2
d0dc53c9941e33a10e7f38ecc0de772f  file3
$ md5sum --check mysum
file1: OK
file2: OK
file3: OK
$ echo "new data" > file2
$ md5sum --check mysum
file1: OK
file2: FAILED
file3: OK
md5sum: WARNING: 1 of 3 computed checksums did NOT match
```

Two different files are highly unlikely to have the same MD5 checksum, so comparing checksums is a reasonably reliable way to detect
if two files differ:

```
$ md5sum myfile1 | cut -c1-32 > sum1
$ md5sum myfile2 | cut -c1-32 > sum2
$ diff -q sum1 sum2
Files sum1 and sum2 differ
```

Some other programs similar to md5sum are sum and cksum, which use
different algorithms to compute their checksums. sum is compatible

---

with other Unix systems, specifically BSD Unix (the default) or System V Unix (-s option), and cksum produces a CRC checksum:

```
$ sum myfile
12410     3
$ sum -s myfile
47909 6 myfile
$ cksum myfile
1204834076 2863 myfile
```

The first integer is a checksum and the second is a block count. But as you can see, these checksums are small numbers and therefore unreliable, since files could have identical checksums by coincidence. md5sum is by far the best. See *http://www.faqs.org/rfcs/rfc1321 .html* for the technical details.

Printing

lpr   Print a file.

lpq   View the print queue.

lprm   Remove a print job from the queue.

Linux has two popular printing systems, called CUPS and LPRng. Both systems use commands with the same names: lpr, lpq, and lprm. However, these commands have different options depending whether you're using CUPS or LPRng. To be generally helpful, we will present common options that work with both systems.

Installing a printer on Linux used to require editing a cryptic configuration file, such as */etc/cups/printers.conf* or */etc/printcap*. Nowadays, both GNOME and KDE have printer configuration tools in their system settings that generate these files.

---

lpr   **stdin**   stdout   - file   -- opt   --help   --version

lpr [*options*] [*files*]

The lpr (line printer) command sends a file to a printer.

```
$ lpr -P myprinter myfile
```

Useful options

-P *printername*	Send the file to printer *printername*, which you have previously set up.
-# *N*	Print *N* copies of the file.
-J *name*	Set the job *name* that prints on the cover page (if your system is set up to print cover pages).

lpq
stdin **stdout** - file -- opt --help --version

lpq [*options*]

The lpq (line printer queue) command lists all print jobs waiting to be printed.

Useful options

-P *printername*	List the queue for printer *printername*.
-a	List the queue for all printers.
-l	Be verbose: display information in a longer format.

lprm
stdin **stdout** - file -- opt --help --version

lprm [*options*] [*job_IDs*]

The lprm (line printer remove) command cancels one or more print jobs. Use lpq to learn the ID of the desired print jobs (say, 61 and 78), then type:

```
$ lprm -P printername 61 78
```

If you don't supply any job IDs, your current print job is canceled. (Only the superuser can cancel other users' jobs.) The -P option specifies which print queue contains the job.

Spell Checking

look   Look up the spelling of a word quickly.

aspell   Interactive spelling checker.

spell   Batch spelling checker.

Linux has several spellcheckers built in. If you're accustomed to graphical spellcheckers, you might find Linux's text-based ones fairly primitive, but they can be used in pipelines, which is quite powerful.

look
stdin   **stdout**   - file   **-- opt**   --help   --version

look [*options*] *prefix* [*dictionary_file*]

The look command prints (on standard output) words that begin with a given string *prefix*. The words are located in a dictionary file (default */usr/share/dict/words*). For instance, look bigg prints:

    bigger
    biggest
    Biggs

If you supply your own dictionary file—any text file with alphabetically sorted lines—look will print all lines beginning with the given *prefix*.

Useful options

-f   Ignore case.

-t *X*   Match the prefix only up to and including the termination character *X*. For instance, look -t i big prints all words beginning with "bi".

aspell
stdin   stdout   - file   **-- opt**   --help   --version

aspell [*options*] *file* | *command*

aspell is a powerful spellchecker with dozens of options. A few useful commands are:

```
aspell -c file
```
> Interactively check, and optionally correct, the spelling of all words in file.

```
aspell -l < file
```
> Print a list of the misspelled words in *file* on standard output.

```
aspell dump master
```
> Print aspell's master dictionary on standard output.

```
aspell help
```
> Print a concise help message. See *http://aspell.net* for more information.

---

spell   stdin   stdout   -file   --opt   --help   --version

```
spell [files]
```

The spell command prints all words in the given files that are misspelled, according to its dictionary.

```
$ spell myfile
thier
naturaly
Linuxx
```

Disks and Filesystems

df   Display available space on mounted filesystems.

mount   Make a disk partition accessible.

umount Unmount a disk partition (make it inaccessible).

fsck   Check a disk partition for errors.

sync   Flush all disk caches to disk.

Linux systems can have multiple disks or disk partitions. In casual conversation, these are variously called disks, partitions, filesystems, volumes, even directories. We'll try to be more accurate.

A *disk* is a hardware device, which may be divided into *partitions* that act as independent storage devices. Partitions are represented on Linux systems as special files in (usually) the directory */dev*. For example, */dev/sda7* could be a partition on your hard drive. Some common devices in */dev* are:

hda	First IDE bus, master device; partitions are *hda1, hda2, ...*
hdb	First IDE bus, slave device; partitions are *hdb1, hdb2, ...*
hdc	Second IDE bus, master device; partitions are *hdc1, hdc2, ...*
hdd	Second IDE bus, slave device; partitions are *hdd1, hdd2, ...*
sda	First block device, such as SCSI, SATA, USB, or Firewire hard drives; partitions are *sda1, sda2, ...*
sdb	Second block device; partitions are *sdb1, sdb2, ...* Likewise for *sdc, sdd, ...*
ht0	First IDE tape drive (then *ht1, ht2, ...*) with auto-rewind
nht0	First IDE tape drive (then *nht1, nht2, ...*) without auto-rewind
st0	First SCSI tape drive (then *st1, st2, ...*)
scd0	First SCSI CD-ROM drive (then *scd1, scd2, ...*)
fd0	First floppy drive (then *fd1, fd2, ...*), usually mounted on */mnt/floppy*

Before a partition can hold files, it is "formatted" by a program that writes a *filesystem* on it (see "Partitioning and Formatting" on page 108). A filesystem defines how files are represented; examples are ext3 (a Linux journaling filesystem) and ntfs (Microsoft Windows NT filesystem). Formatting is generally done for you when you install Linux.

Once a filesystem is created, you can make it available for use by *mounting* it on an empty directory. For example, if you mount a Windows filesystem on a directory */mnt/win*, it becomes part of your system's directory tree, and you can create and edit files like */mnt/win/myfile*. Mounting is generally done automatically at boot time. Filesystems can also be unmounted to make them inaccessible via the filesystem, say, for maintenance.

Partitioning and Formatting

Disk-related operations like partitioning and formatting can be complex on Linux systems. Here are pointers to the programs you may need (start with their manpages).

parted, fdisk, *or* sfdisk

> Partition a hard drive. Any of these programs will do: they simply have different user interfaces.

mkfs

> Format a hard disk, i.e., create a new filesystem.

floppy

> Format a floppy disk.

---

df   stdin **stdout** - file **-- opt** **--help** **--version**

df [*options*] [*disk devices* | *files* | *directories*]

The df (disk free) program shows you the size, used space, and free space on a given disk partition. If you supply a file or directory, df describes the disk device on which that file or directory resides. With no arguments, df reports on all mounted filesystems.

```
$ df
Filesystem      1k-blocks      Used Available Use% Mounted on
/dev/sda        1011928      225464    735060  24% /
/dev/sda9        521748      249148    246096  51% /var
/dev/sda8       8064272     4088636   3565984  54% /usr
/dev/sda10      8064272     4586576   3068044  60% /home
```

Useful options

-k	List sizes in kilobytes (the default).
-m	List sizes in megabytes.
-B *N*	Display sizes in blocks of *N* bytes. (Default = 1024)
-h	Print human-readable output, and choose the most appropriate unit for each size. For example, if your two disks have 1 gigabyte and 25 kilobytes free, respectively, df -h prints 1G and 25K. The -h option uses powers of 1024, whereas -H uses powers of 1000.
-H	

-l	Display only local filesystems, not networked filesystems.
-T	Include the filesystem type (ext3, vfat, etc.) in the output.
-t *type*	Display only filesystems of the given type.
-x *type*	Don't display filesystems of the given type.
-i	Inode mode. Display total, used, and free inodes for each filesystem, instead of disk blocks.

---

mount   stdin   **stdout**   - file   **-- opt**   **--help**   **--version**

mount [*options*] *device* | *directory*

The mount command makes a partition accessible. Most commonly it handles disk drives (say, */dev/sda1*) and removal media (e.g., USB keys), making them accessible via an existing directory (say, */mnt/mydir*):

```
# mkdir /mnt/mydir
# ls /mnt/mydir                    Notice it's empty
# mount /dev/sda1 /mnt/mydir
# ls /mnt/mydir
file1       file2       file3      Files on the mounted partition
# df /mnt/mydir
Filesystem      1K-blocks    Used Available Use% Mounted on
/dev/sda1        1011928   285744    674780  30% /mnt/mydir
```

mount has tons of options and uses; we will discuss only the most basic.

In most common cases, mount reads the file */etc/fstab* (filesystem table) to learn how to mount a desired disk. For example, if you type mount */usr*, the mount command looks up "/usr" in */etc/fstab*, whose line might look like this:

```
/dev/sda8    /usr    ext3    defaults    1    2
```

Here mount learns, among other things, that disk device */dev/sda8* should be mounted on */usr* as a Linux ext3-formatted filesystem. Now you can mount */dev/sda8* on */usr* with either of these commands:

```
# mount /dev/sda8    by device
# mount /usr         by directory
```

---

mount is run typically by the superuser, but common devices like USB and CD-ROM drives often can be mounted and unmounted by any user.

```
$ mount /media/cdrom
```

Useful options

-t *type*   Specify the type of filesystem, such as ext3 or ntfs.

-l   List all mounted filesystems; works with -t too.

-a   Mount all filesystems listed in */etc/fstab*. Ignores entries that include the noauto option. Works well with -t too.

-r   Mount the filesystem read-only (but see the manpage for some disclaimers).

---

umount   stdin   **stdout**   - file   **-- opt**   --help   --version

umount [*options*] [*device* | *directory*]

umount does the opposite of mount: it makes a disk partition unavailable via the filesystem. For instance, if you've mounted a CD-ROM disc, you can't eject it until it's umounted:

```
$ umount /media/cdrom
```

Always unmount a removable medium before ejecting it or you risk damage to its filesystem. To unmount all mounted devices:

```
# umount -a
```

Don't unmount a filesystem that's in use; in fact, the umount command will refuse to do so for safety reasons.

---

fsck   stdin   **stdout**   - file   **-- opt**   --help   --version

fsck [*options*] [*devices*]

The fsck (filesystem check) command validates a Linux disk partition and, if requested, repairs errors found on it. fsck is run automatically when your system boots; however, you can run it manually if you like. In general, unmount a device before checking it, so no other programs are operating on it at the same time:

```
# umount /dev/sda10
# fsck -f /dev/sda10
Pass 1: Checking inodes, blocks, and sizes
Pass 2: Checking directory structure
Pass 3: Checking directory connectivity
Pass 4: Checking reference counts
Pass 5: Checking group summary information
/home: 172/1281696 files (11.6% non-contiguous), ...
```

fsck is a frontend for a set of filesystem-checking programs found
in */sbin*, with names beginning "fsck". Only certain types of filesystems are supported; you can list them with the command:

```
$ ls /sbin/fsck.* | cut -d. -f2
```

Useful options

-A   Check all disks listed in */etc/fstab*, in order.

-N   Print a description of the checking that would be done, but exit without performing
      any checking.

-r   Fix errors interactively, prompting before each fix.

-a   Fix errors automatically (use only if you *really* know what you're doing; if not, you
      can seriously mess up a filesystem).

---

sync   stdin   stdout   - file   -- opt   **--help**   **--version**

sync

The sync command flushes all disk caches to disk. The kernel usually buffers reads, writes, inode changes, and other disk-related ac-
tivity in memory. sync writes the changes to disk. Normally, you
don't need to run this command, but if (say) you're about to do
something risky that might crash your machine, running sync immediately beforehand can't hurt.

Backups and Remote Storage

dump   Write a disk partition to a backup medium.

restore   Restore the results of a dump.

cdrecord Burn a CD, DVD, or Blu-ray disc.

| rsync | Mirror a set of files onto another device or host. |
| mt | Control a tape drive. |

There are various way to back up your precious Linux files:

- Copy them to a backup medium, such as an external hard drive.
- Burn them onto a writeable CD, DVD, or Blu-ray disc.
- Mirror them to a remote machine.

We aren't presenting every available Linux command for backups. Some users prefer cpio, and for low-level disk copies, dd is invaluable. See the manpages for these programs if you are interested in them.

---

dump
stdin **stdout**   **- file**   -- opt   --help   --version

dump [*options*] *partition_or_files*

The dump command writes an entire disk partition, or selected files, to a backup medium such as tape. It supports full and incremental backups, automatically figuring out which files need to be backed up (i.e., which have changed since the last backup). To restore files from the backup medium, use the restore command.

To perform a full backup of a given filesystem (say, */usr*) to your backup device (say, */dev/tape*), use the -0 (zero) and -u options:

```
# dump -0 -u -f /dev/tape /usr
```

This is called a *level zero* dump. The -u option writes a note to the file */etc/dumpdates* to say that the backup was performed.

Incremental backups may have levels 1 through 9: a level *i* backup stores all new and changed files since the last level *i-1* backup.

```
# dump -1 -u -f /dev/tape /usr
```

Don't run dump on a "live" filesystem actively in use: unmount it first when possible.

restore [*options*] [*files*]

The restore command reads a backup created by dump. It can then restore the files to disk, compare them against those on disk, and other operations. The friendliest way to use restore is with the -i flag for interactive operation, which lets you browse the dumped contents just like a filesystem, selecting files and directories, and finally restoring them.

```
# restore -i -f /dev/tape
```

restore then prompts you for commands like the ones listed below.

help	Print a help message.
quit	Exit the program without restoring any files.
cd *dir*	Like the shell's cd command, set your current working directory within the dump for working with files.
ls	Like the Linux ls command, view all files in the current working directory within the dump.
pwd	Like the shell's pwd command, print the name of your current working directory within the dump.
add	Add files or directories to the "extraction list": the list of files you'll want to restore. With no arguments, add adds the current directory and all its files.
add *file*	Add the file to the extraction list.
add *dir*	Add the directory *dir* to the extraction list.
delete	The opposite of add: remove files from the extraction list. If run with no arguments, delete removes the current directory (and its contents) from the extraction list.
delete *file*	Remove the file from the extraction list.
delete *dir*	Remove the directory *dir* from the extraction list.
extract	Restore all the files you added to the extraction list. (Tip: if your backup spans multiple tapes, start with the last tape and work backward.)

restore also works in other noninteractive modes:

restore -x	Restore everything from the backup into an existing filesystem. (cd into the root of the desired filesystem first.)
restore -r	Restore everything from the backup into a freshly formatted disk partition. (cd into the root of the desired filesystem first.)
restore -t	List the contents of the dump.
restore -C	Compare the dump against the original filesystem.

---

cdrecord

stdin   stdout   - file   -- opt   --help   --version

```
cdrecord [options] tracks
```

The cdrecord command burns a writable CD, DVD, or Blu-ray disc.
To burn the contents of a Linux directory onto a disc readable on
Linux, Windows, and Macintosh systems:[14]

1. Locate your disc writer's device by running:

   ```
   $ cdrecord --scanbus
   ...
   0,0,0   0) *
   0,1,0   1) *
   0,2,0   2) *
   0,3,0   3) 'YAMAHA  ' 'CRW6416S  ' '1.0d' CD-ROM
   ...
   ```

   The device in this case is 0,3,0.

2. Find out your CD writer's speed for writing CD-R or CD-RW
   discs (whichever you're using). Suppose it is a 6x writer of
   CD-Rs, so the speed is 6.

3. Put the files you want to burn into a directory, say, *dir*. Arrange
   them exactly as you'd like them on the CD. The directory *dir*
   itself will not be copied to CD, just its contents.

4. Burn the CD:

   ```
   $ DEVICE="0,3,0"
   $ SPEED=6
   $ mkisofs -R -l dir > mydisk.iso
   $ cdrecord -v dev=${DEVICE} speed=${SPEED} mydisk.iso
   ```

---

14. Specifically, an ISO9660 CD with Rock Ridge extensions. mkisofs can
create other formats for cdrecord to burn: see man mkisofs.

or if your system is fast enough, you can do this with a single pipeline:

```
$ mkisofs -R -l dir \
    | cdrecord -v dev=${DEVICE} speed=${SPEED} -
```

cdrecord can burn music CDs as well, but you might want to use a friendlier, graphical program like k3b instead (see "Audio" on page 185), which is built on top of cdrecord.

---

rsync

stdin   **stdout** - file **-- opt** **--help** **--version**

```
rsync [options] source destination
```

The rsync command copies a set of files. It can make an exact copy, including file permissions and other attributes (called *mirroring*), or it can just copy the data. It can run over a network or on a single machine. rsync has many uses and over 50 options; we'll present just a few common cases relating to backups.

To mirror the directory *D1* and its contents into another directory *D2* on a single machine:

```
$ rsync -a D1 D2
```

In order to mirror directory *D1* over the network to another host, *server.example.com*, where you have an account with username smith, secure the connection with SSH to prevent eavesdropping:

```
$ rsync -a -e ssh D1 smith@server.example.com:D2
```

Useful options

-o	Copy the ownership of the files. (You might need superuser privileges on the remote host.)
-g	Copy the group ownership of the files. (You might need superuser privileges on the remote host.)
-p	Copy the file permissions.
-t	Copy the file timestamps.
-r	Copy directories recursively, i.e., including their contents.
-l	Permit symbolic links to be copied (not the files they point to).
-D	Permit devices to be copied. (Superuser only.)

-a	Mirroring: copy all attributes of the original files. This implies all of the options, -ogptrlD.
-v	Verbose mode: print information about what's happening during the copy. Add --progress to display a numeric progress meter while files are copied.
-e ssh	Connect via ssh for more security. (Other remote shells are possible, but ssh is the most common.)

---

mt   stdin **stdout** - file -- opt **--help** **--version**

```
mt [-f device] command
```

The mt (magnetic tape) command performs simple operations on a tape drive, such as rewinding, skipping forward and backward, and retensioning. Some common operations are:

status	Show the status of the drive.
rewind	Rewind the tape.
retension	Retension the tape.
erase	Erase the tape.
offline	Take the tape drive offline.
eod	Move forward on the tape to the end of data.

For example:

```
$ mt -f /dev/tape rewind
```

You can also move through the tape, file by file or record by record, but often you'll use a tape reading/writing program for that, such as tar or restore.

Viewing Processes

ps	List process.
uptime	View the system load.
w	List active processes for all users.
top	Monitor resource-intensive processes interactively.

`gnome-system-monitor`	Monitor system load and processes graphically.
`xload`	Simple, graphical monitor of system load.
`free`	Display free memory.

A *process* is a unit of work on a Linux system. Each program you run represents one or more processes, and Linux provides commands for viewing and manipulating them. Every process is identified by a numeric *process ID*, or PID.

Processes are different from jobs (see "Shell Job Control" on page 32): processes are part of the operating system, whereas jobs are higher-level constructs known only to the shell in which they're running. A running program comprises one or more processes; a job consists of one or more programs executed as a shell command.

---

ps   stdin   **stdout**   - file   -- opt   **--help**   **--version**

`ps [options]`

The `ps` command displays information about your running processes, and optionally the processes of other users.

```
$ ps
   PID TTY          TIME CMD
  4706 pts/2    00:00:01 bash
 15007 pts/2    00:00:00 emacs
 16729 pts/2    00:00:00 ps
```

ps has at least 80 options; we'll cover just a few useful combinations. If the options seem arbitrary or inconsistent, it's because the supplied ps command (GNU ps) incorporates the features of several other Unix ps commands, attempting to be compatible with all of them.

To view your processes:

```
$ ps -ux
```

all of user smith's processes:

```
$ ps -U smith
```

---

all occurrences of a program:

```
$ ps -C program_name
```

processes on terminal *N*:

```
$ ps -tN
```

particular processes 1, 2, and 3505:

```
$ ps -p1,2,3505
```

all processes with command lines truncated to screen width:

```
$ ps -ef
```

all processes with full command lines:

```
$ ps -efww
```

and all processes in a threaded view, which indents child processes below their parents:

```
$ ps -efH
```

Remember, you can extract information more finely from the output of ps using grep and other filter programs:

```
$ ps -ux | grep myprogram
```

---

uptime   stdin **stdout** - file -- opt --help --version

```
uptime
```

The uptime command tells you how long the system has been running since the last boot.

```
$ uptime
 10:54pm  up 8 days,  3:44,  3 users,  load average: 0.89,
 1.00, 2.15
```

This information is, from left to right: the current time (10:54pm), system uptime (8 days, 3 hours, 44 minutes), number of users logged in (3), and system load average for three time periods: one minute (0.89), five minutes (1.00), and fifteen minutes (2.15). The load average is the average number of processes ready to run in that time interval.

w [*username*]

The w command displays the current process running in each shell
for all logged-in users:

```
$ w
 10:51pm  up 8 days,  3:42,  8 users,
 load average: 0.00, 0.00, 0.00
 USER    TTY   FROM  LOGIN@  IDLE    JCPU   PCPU  WHAT
 barrett pts/0 :0    Sat 2pm 27:13m 0.07s  0.07s emacs
 jones   pts/1 host1 6Sep03   2:33m 0.74s  0.21s bash
 smith   pts/2 host2 6Sep03   0.00s 13.35s 0.04s w
```

The top line is the same one printed by uptime. The columns indicate the user's terminal, originating host or X display (if applicable),
login time, idle time, two measures of the CPU time (run man w for
details), and the current process. Provide a username to see only
that user's information.

For the briefest output, try w -hfs.

Useful options

-h   Don't print the header line.

-f   Don't print the FROM column.

-s   Don't print the JCPU and PCPU columns.

---

top [*options*]

The top command lets you monitor the most active processes, up-
dating the display at regular intervals (say, every second). It is a
screen-based program that updates the display in place,
interactively.

```
$ top
94 processes: 81 sleeping, 1 running, 0 zombie, 11 stopped
CPU states: 1.1% user, 0.5% system, 0.0% nice, 4.5% idle
Mem: 523812K av, 502328K used, 21484K free, 0K shrd, ...
Swap: 530104K av, 0K used, 530104K free  115300K cached
```

```
PID   USER PRI NI SIZE SHARE STAT %CPU %MEM TIME COMMAND
26265 smith 10 0 1092  840  R    4.7  0.2 0:00 top
    1 root   0 0  540  472  S    0.0  0.1 0:07 init
    2 root   0 0    0    0  SW   0.0  0.0 0:00 kflushd
...
```

While top is running, you can press keys to change its behavior, such as setting the update speed (s), hiding idle processes (i), or killing processes (k). Type h to see a complete list and q to quit.

Useful options

-n*N*	Perform *N* updates, then quit.
-d*N*	Update the display every *N* seconds.
-p*N* -p*M* ...	Display only the processes with PID *N*, *M*, ..., up to 20 processes.
-c	Display the command-line arguments of processes.
-b	Print on standard output noninteractively, without playing screen tricks. top -b -n1 > outfile saves a quick snapshot to a file.

---

gnome-system-monitor   stdin stdout - file -- opt **--help** --version

gnome-system-monitor

gnome-system-monitor is a graphical tool that displays the system load of each processor, a list of running processes, and information on memory, filesystems, and more.

---

xload   stdin   stdout   - file   -- opt   --help   --version

xload

xload is a very simple monitoring tool that graphs processor load (Y axis) over time (X axis). If your computer has multiple processors or cores, xload does not provide separate views, and you'll probably prefer a more powerful tool like gnome-system-monitor.

Useful options

-update *N*	Update the display every *N* seconds (default 10).

-scale N	Divide the Y axis into N sections (default 1). xload may add more divisions as the load goes up; N is the minimum visible at any time.
-hl color	Use this color for the scale divider lines.
-label X	Print the text X above the graph (default = your hostname).
-nolabel	Don't print any text label above the graph.
-jumpscroll N	When the graph reaches the right margin, scroll N pixels to the left and keep drawing (default is half the window width).

---

free

stdin   **stdout**   - file   -- opt   **--help**   **--version**

```
free [options]
```

The free command displays memory usage in kilobytes:

```
$ free
             total      used      free shared buffers cached
Mem:        523812    491944     31868      0   67856 199276
-/+ buffers/cache: 224812    299000
Swap:       530104         0    530104
```

The Linux kernel reserves as much memory as possible for caching purposes, so your best estimate of free RAM in the preceding output is in the buffers/cache row, free column (i.e., 299000K).

Useful options

-s N	Run continuously and update the display every N seconds.
-b	Display amounts in bytes.
-m	Display amounts in megabytes.
-t	Add a totals row at the bottom.
-o	Don't display the "buffers/cache" row.

Controlling Processes

kill	Terminate a process (or send it a signal).
nice	Invoke a program at a particular priority.
renice	Change a process's priority as it runs.

Once processes are started, they can be stopped, restarted, killed, and reprioritized. We discussed some of these operations as handled by the shell in "Shell Job Control" on page 32. Now we cover killing and reprioritizing.

---

kill

stdin   stdout   - file   -- opt   --help   --version

```
kill [options] [process_ids]
```

The kill command sends a signal to a process. This can terminate a process (the default action), interrupt it, suspend it, crash it, and so on. You must own the process, or be the superuser, to affect it. To terminate process 13243, for example, run:

```
$ kill 13243
```

If this does not work—some programs catch this signal without terminating—add the -KILL or (equivalently) -9 option:

```
$ kill -KILL 13243
```

which is virtually guaranteed to work. However, this is not a clean exit for the program, which may leave resources allocated (or cause other inconsistencies) upon its death.

If you don't know the PID of a process, run ps and examine the output:

```
$ ps -uax | grep emacs
```

or even better, try the pidof command, which looks up and prints the PID of a process by its name:

```
$ pidof emacs
8374
```

Now you can kill a process knowing only its program name in a single line, using shell backquotes to execute pidof:

```
$ kill `pidof emacs`
```

In addition to the kill program in the filesystem (usually */bin/kill*), most shells have built-in kill commands, but their syntax and behavior differ. However, they all support the following usage:

```
$ kill -N PID
$ kill -NAME PID
```

---

where *N* is a signal number, and *NAME* is a signal name without its leading "SIG" (e.g., use -HUP to send the SIGHUP signal). To see a complete list of signals transmitted by kill, run kill -1, though its output differs depending on which kill you're running. For descriptions of the signals, run man 7 signal.

---

nice

stdin   **stdout**   - file   -- opt   **--help**   **--version**

```
nice [-level] command_line
```

When invoking a system-intensive program, you can be nice to the other processes (and users) by lowering its priority. That's what the nice command is for: it sets a *nice level* (an amount of "niceness") for a process so it gets less attention from the Linux process scheduler.[15] Here's an example of setting a big job to run at nice level 7:

```
$ nice -7 sort VeryLargeFile > outfile
```

If you run nice without a level, 10 is used. Normal processes (run without nice) run at level zero, which you can see by running nice with no arguments:

```
$ nice
0
```

The superuser can also lower the nice level, increasing a process's priority:

```
# nice --10 myprogram
```

(Yes, that's "dash negative 10".) To see the nice levels of your jobs, use ps and look at the "NI" column:

```
$ ps -o pid,user,args,nice
```

---

renice

stdin   **stdout**   - file   -- opt   --help   --version

```
renice [+-N] [options] PID
```

While the nice command can invoke a program at a given nice level, renice changes the nice level of an already-running process. Here

---

15. This is called "nicing" the process. You'll hear the term used as a verb: "That process was niced to 12."

Controlling Processes | 123

we increase the nice level (decrease the priority) of process 28734 by five:

```
$ renice +5 -p 28734
```

Ordinary users can increase the nice level of their own processes, while the superuser can also decrease it (increasing the priority) and can operate on any process. The valid range is –20 to +20, but avoid high negative numbers or you might interfere with vital system processes.

Useful options

-p *pid*   Affect the given process ID. You can omit the -p and just provide a PID (renice +5 28734).

-u *username*   Affect all processes owned by the given user.

Scheduling Jobs

sleep   Wait a set number of seconds, doing nothing.

watch   Run a program at set intervals.

at   Schedule a job for a single, future time.

crontab   Schedule jobs for many future times.

If you need to launch programs at particular times or at regular intervals, Linux provides several scheduling tools at various degrees of complexity.

---

sleep   stdin   stdout   - file   -- opt   **--help**   **--version**

sleep *time_specification*

The sleep command simply waits a set amount of time. The given time specification can be an integer (meaning seconds) or an integer followed by the letter s (also seconds), m (minutes), h (hours), or d (days).

```
$ sleep 5m
```
                    Do nothing for 5 minutes

sleep is useful for delaying a command for a set amount of time:

```
$ sleep 10 && echo 'Ten seconds have passed.'
(10 seconds pass)
Ten seconds have passed.
```

---

watch   stdin   **stdout**   - file   **-- opt**   **--help**   **--version**

watch [*options*] *command*

The watch program executes a given command at regular intervals;
the default is every two seconds. The command is passed to the shell
(so be sure to quote or escape any special characters), and the results
are displayed in a full-screen mode, so you can observe the output
conveniently and see what has changed. For example, watch -n 60
date executes the date command once a minute, sort of a poor man's
clock. Type ^C to exit.

Useful options

-n *seconds*	Set the time between executions, in seconds.
-d	Highlight differences in the output, to emphasize what has changed from one execution to the next.

---

at   **stdin**   **stdout**   - file   **-- opt**   --help   --version

at [*options*] *time_specification*

The at command runs a shell command once at a specified time:

```
$ at 7am next sunday
at> echo Remember to go shopping | mail smith
at> lpr $HOME/shopping-list
at> ^D
<EOT>
job 559 at 2011-09-14 21:30
```

The time specifications understood by at are enormously flexible.
In general, you can specify:

* A time followed by a date (not a date followed by a time)

* Only a date (assumes the current clock time)

* Only a time (assumes the very next occurrence, whether today
  or tomorrow)

- A special word like now, midnight, or teatime (16:00)
- Any of the preceding followed by an offset, like "+ 3 days"

Dates are acceptable in many forms: december 25 2012, 25 december 2012, december 25, 25 december, 12/25/2012, 25.12.2012, 20121225, today, thursday, next thursday, next month, next year, and more. Month names can be abbreviated to three letters (jan, feb, mar, ...). Times are also flexible: 8pm, 8 pm, 8:00pm, 8:00 pm, 20:00, and 2000 are equivalent. Offsets are a plus or minus sign followed by white-space and an amount of time: + 3 seconds, + 2 weeks, - 1 hour, and so on.[16]

If you don't specify a part of the date or time, at copies the missing information from the system date and time. So "next year" means one year from right now, "thursday" means the upcoming Thursday at the current clock time, "december 25" means the next upcoming December 25, and "4:30pm" means the very next occurrence of 4:30 p.m. in the future.

The command you supply to at is not evaluated by the shell until execution time, so wildcards, variables, and other shell constructs are not expanded until then. Also, your current environment (see printenv) is preserved within each job so it executes as if you were logged in. Aliases, however, aren't available to at jobs, so don't include them.

To list your at jobs, use atq ("at queue"):

```
$ atq
559   2011-09-14 07:00 a smith
```

To delete an at job, run atrm ("at remove") with the job number:

```
$ atrm 559
```

Useful options

-f *filename*	Read commands from the given file instead of standard input.
-c *job_number*	Print the job commands to standard output.

16. Programmers can read the precise syntax in */usr/share/doc/at/timespec*.

crontab [*options*] [*file*]

The crontab command, like at, schedules jobs for specific times. However, crontab is for recurring jobs, such as "Run this command at midnight on the second Tuesday of each month." To make this work, you edit and save a file (called your *crontab file*), which automatically gets installed in a system directory (*/var/spool/cron*). Once a minute, a Linux process called cron wakes up, checks your crontab file, and executes any jobs that are due.

$ crontab -e
> Edit your crontab file in your default editor ($EDITOR)

$ crontab -l
> Print your crontab file on standard output

$ crontab -r
> Delete your crontab file

$ crontab myfile
> Install the file *myfile* as your crontab file

The superuser can add the option -u *username* to work with other users' crontab files.

Crontab files contain one job per line. (Blank lines and comment lines beginning with "#" are ignored.) Each line has six fields, separated by whitespace. The first five fields specify the time to run the job, and the last is the job command itself.

Minutes of the hour
> Integers between 0 and 59. This can be a single number (30), a sequence of numbers separated by commas (0,15,30,45), a range (20-30), a sequence of ranges (0-15,50-59), or an asterisk to mean "all." You can also specify "every *n*th time" with the suffix /*n*; for instance, both */12 and 0-59/12 mean 0,12,24,36,48 (i.e., every 12 minutes).

Hours of the day
> Same syntax as for minutes.

Days of the month
> Integers between 1 and 31; again, you may use sequences, ranges, sequences of ranges, or an asterisk.

Months of the year
> Integers between 1 and 12; again, you may use sequences, ranges, sequences of ranges, or an asterisk. Additionally, you may use three-letter abbreviations (jan, feb, mar, ...), but not in ranges or sequences.

Days of the week
> Integers between 0 (Sunday) and 6 (Saturday); again, you may use sequences, ranges, sequences of ranges, or an asterisk. Additionally, you may use three-letter abbreviations (sun, mon, tue, ...), but not in ranges or sequences.

Command to execute
> Any shell command, which will be executed in your login environment, so you can refer to environment variables like $HOME and expect them to work. Use only absolute paths to your commands (e.g., */usr/bin/who* instead of who) as a general rule.

Some example time specifications are:

*	*	*	*	*	Every minute
45	*	*	*	*	45 minutes after each hour (1:45, 2:45, etc.)
45	9	*	*	*	Every day at 9:45 am
45	9	8	*	*	The eighth day of every month at 9:45 am
45	9	8	12	*	Every December 8 at 9:45 am
45	9	8	dec	*	Every December 8 at 9:45 am
45	9	*	*	6	Every Saturday at 9:45 am
45	9	*	*	sat	Every Saturday at 9:45 am
45	9	*	12	6	Every Saturday in December, at 9:45 am
45	9	8	12	6	Every Saturday in December, plus December 8, at 9:45 am

If the command produces any output upon execution, cron will email it to you.

Logins, Logouts, and Shutdowns

We assume you know how to log into your Linux account. To log out using GNOME or KDE, choose Logout from the main menu. To log out from a remote shell, just close the shell (type exit or logout).

Never simply turn off the power to a Linux system: it needs a more graceful shutdown. To perform a shutdown from GNOME or KDE, use the main menu. To perform a shutdown from a shell, run the shutdown command as the superuser, as follows.

---

shutdown   stdin   **stdout**   - file   -- opt   --help   --version

shutdown [*options*] *time* [*message*]

The shutdown command halts or reboots a Linux system; only the superuser may run it. Here's a command to halt the system in 10 minutes, broadcasting the message "scheduled maintenance" to all users logged in:

    # shutdown -h +10 "scheduled maintenance"

The *time* may be a number of minutes preceded by a plus sign, like +10; an absolute time in hours and minutes, like 16:25; or the word now to mean immediately.

With no options, shutdown puts the system into single-user mode, a special maintenance mode in which only one person is logged in (at the system console), and all nonessential services are off. To exit single-user mode, either perform another shutdown to halt or reboot, or type ^D to bring up the system in normal, multiuser mode.

Useful options

- -r   Reboot the system.

- -h   Halt the system.

- -k   Kidding: don't really perform a shutdown, just broadcast warning messages to all users as if the system were going down.

- -c   Cancel a shutdown in progress (omit the *time* argument).

- -f   On reboot, skip the usual filesystem check performed by the fsck program (described in "Disks and Filesystems" on page 106).

- -F   On reboot, require the usual filesystem check.

For technical information about shutdowns, single-user mode, and various system states, see the manpages for init and inittab.

Users and Their Environment

logname	Print your login name.
whoami	Print your current, effective username.
id	Print the user ID and group membership of a user.
who	List logged-in users, long output.
users	List logged-in users, short output.
finger	Print information about users.
last	Determine when someone last logged in.
printenv	Print your environment.

Who are you? Only the system knows for sure. This grab-bag of programs tells you all about *users*: their names, login times, and properties of their environment.

---

logname   stdin **stdout** - file -- opt **--help** **--version**

logname

The logname command prints your login name. It might seem trivial, but it's useful in shell scripts.

```
$ logname
smith
```

---

whoami

stdin   **stdout**   - file   -- opt   **--help**   **--version**

whoami

The whoami command prints the name of the current, effective user. This may differ from your login name (the output of logname) if you've used the su command. This example distinguishes whoami from logname:

```
$ logname
smith
$ whoami
smith

$ su
Password: ********
# logname
smith
# whoami
root
```

id

stdin   **stdout**   - file   -- opt   **--help**   **--version**

id [*options*] [*username*]

Every user has a unique, numeric *user ID*, and a default group with a unique, numeric *group ID*. The id command prints these values along with their associated user and group names:

```
$ id
uid=500(smith) gid=500(smith)
groups=500(smith),6(disk),490(src),501(cdwrite)
```

Useful options

-u   Print the effective user ID and exit.

-g   Print the effective group ID and exit.

-G   Print the IDs of all other groups to which the user belongs.

-n   Print names (for users and groups) rather than numeric IDs. Must be combined with -u, -g, or -G. For example, id -Gn produces the same output as the groups command.

-r   Print login values instead of effective values. Must be combined with -u, -g, or -G.

who
stdin   **stdout**   - file   -- opt   **--help**   **--version**

who [*options*] [*filename*]

The who command lists all logged-in users, one user shell per line:

```
$ who
smith     pts/0    Sep  6 17:09 (:0)
barrett   pts/1    Sep  6 17:10 (10.24.19.240)
jones     pts/2    Sep  8 20:58 (192.168.13.7)
jones     pts/4    Sep  3 05:11 (192.168.13.7)
```

Normally, who gets its data from the file */var/run/utmp*. The *file name* argument can specify a different data file, such as */var/log/wtmp* for past logins or */var/log/btmp* for failed logins.[17]

Useful options

-H	Print a row of headings as the first line.
--lookup	For remotely logged-in users, print the hostnames of origin.
-u	Also print each user's idle time at his/her terminal.
-T	Also indicate whether each user's terminal is writable (see mesg in "Instant Messaging" on page 166). A plus sign means yes, a minus sign means no, and a question mark means unknown.
-m	Display information only about yourself, i.e., the user associated with the current terminal.
-q	Quick display of usernames only, and a count of users. Much like the users command, but it adds a count.

users
stdin   **stdout**   - file   -- opt   **--help**   **--version**

users [*filename*]

The users command prints a quick listing of users who have login sessions. If a user is running multiple shells, she appears multiple times.

```
$ users
barrett jones smith smith smith
```

17. If your system is configured to log this information.

Like the who command, users reads */var/log/utmp* by default but can read from another supplied file instead.

finger

```
finger [options] [user[@host]]
```

The finger command prints logged-in user information in a short form:

```
$ finger
Login     Name             Tty       Idle  Login Time
smith     Sandy Smith      :0              Sep  6 17:09
barrett   Daniel Barrett   :pts/1    24    Sep  6 17:10
jones     Jill Jones       :pts/2          Sep  8 20:58
```

or a long form:

```
$ finger smith
Login: smith                         Name: Sandy Smith
Directory: /home/smith               Shell: /bin/bash
On since Sat Sep  6 17:09 (EDT) on :0
Last login Mon Sep  8 21:07 (EDT) on pts/6 from localhost
No mail.
Project:
Enhance world peace
Plan:
Mistrust first impulses; they are always right.
```

The *user* argument can be a local username or a remote user in the form *user@host*. Remote hosts will respond to finger requests only if they are configured to do so.

Useful options

-l   Print in long format.

-s   Print in short format.

-p   Don't display the Project and Plan sections, which are ordinarily read from the user's ~/.*project* and ~/.*plan* files, respectively.

last

last [*options*] [*users*] [*ttys*]

The last command displays a history of logins, in reverse chrono-
logical order.

```
$ last
barrett  pts/3  localhost  Mon Sep 8 21:07 - 21:08 (00:01)
smith    pts/6  :0         Mon Sep 8 20:25 - 20:56 (00:31)
barrett  pts/4  myhost     Sun Sep 7 22:19 still logged in
...
```

You may provide usernames or tty names to limit the output.

Useful options

-*N*	Print only the latest *N* lines of output, where *N* is a positive integer.
-i	Display IP addresses instead of hostnames.
-R	Don't display hostnames.
-x	Also display system shutdowns and changes in system runlevel (e.g., from single-user mode into multiuser mode).
-f *filename*	Read from some other data file than */var/run/wtmp*; see the who command for more details.

---

printenv

printenv [*environment_variables*]

The printenv command prints all environment variables known to
your shell and their values:

```
$ printenv
HOME=/home/smith
MAIL=/var/spool/mail/smith
NAME=Sandy Smith
SHELL=/bin/bash
...
```

or only specified variables:

```
$ printenv HOME SHELL
/home/smith
/bin/bash
```

User Account Management

useradd	Create an account.
userdel	Delete an account.
usermod	Modify an account.
passwd	Change a password.
chfn	Change a user's personal information.
chsh	Change a user's shell.

The installation process for your Linux distro undoubtedly prompted you to create a superuser account (root), and possibly also an ordinary user account (presumably for yourself). But you might want to create other accounts, too.

Creating users is an important job not to be taken lightly. Every account is a potential avenue for an intruder to enter your system, so every user should have a strong, hard-to-guess password.

---

useradd

stdin **stdout** - file **-- opt** --help --version

useradd [*options*] *username*

The useradd command lets the superuser create a user account.

    # useradd smith

Its defaults are not very useful (run useradd -D to see them), so be sure to supply all desired options. For example:

    # useradd -d /home/smith -s /bin/bash -g users smith

Useful options

-d *dir*	Set the user's home directory to be *dir*.
-s *shell*	Set the user's login shell to be *shell*.
-u *uid*	Set the user's ID to be *uid*. Unless you know what you're doing, omit this option and accept the default.
-c *string*	Set the user's comment field (historically called the

	GECOS field). This is usually the user's full name, but it can be any string. The chfn command can also set this information.
-g *group*	Set the user's initial (default) group to *group*, which can either be a numeric group ID or a group name, and which must already exist.
-G *group1,group2,...*	Make the user a member of the additional, existing groups *group1*, *group2*, and so on.
-m	Copy all files from your system skeleton directory, */etc/skel*, into the newly created home directory. The skeleton directory traditionally contains minimal (skeletal) versions of initialization files, like *~/.bash_profile*, to get new users started. If you prefer to copy from a different directory, add the -k option (-k *dirname*).

---

userdel   stdin   **stdout**   - file   **-- opt**   --help   --version

userdel [-r] *username*

The userdel command deletes an existing user.

    # userdel smith

It does not delete the files in the user's home directory unless you supply the -r option. Think carefully before deleting a user; consider deactivating the account instead (with usermod -L). And make sure you have backups of all the user's files before deleting them: you might need them again someday.

---

usermod   stdin   **stdout**   - file   **-- opt**   --help   --version

usermod [*options*] *username*

The usermod command modifies the given user's account in various ways, such as changing a home directory:

    # usermod -d /home/another smith

Useful options

-d *dir*   Change the user's home directory to *dir*.

`-l username`	Change the user's login name to *username*. Think carefully before doing this, in case anything on your system depends on the original name. And don't change system accounts (root, daemon, and so on) unless you really know what you're doing!
`-s shell`	Change the user's login shell to *shell*.
`-g group`	Change the user's initial (default) group to *group*, which can either be a numeric group ID or a group name, and which must already exist.
`-G group1,group2,...`	Make the user a member *only* of the additional, existing groups *group1*, *group2*, and so on. If the user previously belonged to other groups, but you don't specify them here, the user will no longer belong to them.
`-L`	Disable (lock) the account so the user cannot log in.
`-U`	Unlock the account after a lock (`-L`) operation.

---

passwd

stdin **stdout** - file **-- opt** **--help** --version

`passwd [options] [username]`

The passwd command changes a login password, yours by default:

    $ passwd

or another user's password if run by the superuser:

    # passwd smith

passwd does have options, most of them related to password expiration. Use them only in the context of a well-thought-out security policy.

---

chfn

stdin **stdout** - file **-- opt** **--help** **--version**

`chfn [options] [username]`

The chfn (change finger) command updates a few pieces of personal information maintained by the system: real name, home telephone, office telephone, and office location, as displayed by the finger command. Invoked without a username, chfn affects your account;

invoked with a username (by root), it affects that user. With no options, chfn will prompt you for the desired information.

```
$ chfn
Password: ********
Name [Shawn Smith]: Shawn E. Smith
Office [100 Barton Hall]:
Office Phone [212-555-1212]: 212-555-1234
Home Phone []:
```

Useful options

-f name	Change the full name to *name*.
-h phone	Change the home phone number to *phone*.
-p phone	Change the office phone number to *phone*.
-o office	Change the office location to *office*.

---

chsh   stdin   **stdout**   - file   -- opt   --help   --version

chsh [*options*] [*username*]

The chsh (change shell) command sets your login shell program. Invoked without a username, chsh affects your account; invoked with a username (by root), it affects that user. With no options, chsh will prompt you for the desired information.

```
$ chsh
Changing shell for smith.
Password: ********
New shell [/bin/bash]: /bin/tcsh
```

The new shell must be listed in */etc/shells*.

Useful options

-s shell	Specify the new shell.
-l	List all permissible shells.

Becoming the Superuser

Normal users, for the most part, can modify only the files they own. One special user, called the *superuser* or *root*, has full access to the machine and can do anything on it. To become the superuser, log in as yourself and type:

```
$ su -l
Password: *******
#
```

You will be prompted for the superuser password (which we presume you know, if it's your computer). Your shell prompt will change to a hash mark (#) to indicate you are the superuser. When finished executing commands as the superuser, type ^D or run **exit** to end the superuser shell and become yourself again.

If you provide a username to **su**:

```
$ su -l sophia
Password: ********
```

you can become that user (provided you know her password).

---

sudo

su is the simplest way to obtain superuser privileges. A more complex program, **sudo**, runs one command at a time as the superuser, using *your own* password, if your system is configured to use it:

```
$ sudo rm protected_file
Password: ********          Your own password
```

sudo is superior for systems with multiple superusers, as it provides precise control over privileges (in the */etc/sudoers* file) and even logs the commands that get run. A full discussion is beyond the scope of this book: see man **sudo** and *http://www.gratisoft.us/sudo/* for full details.

Useful options

-l	Run a login shell. You almost always want this option, so root's proper search path is set.
-m	Preserve your current environment variables in the new shell.
-c *command*	Run just this *command* (as the other user) and exit. If you need to do this a lot, read the sudo manpage.
-s *shell*	Run the given shell (e.g., */bin/bash*).

Group Management

groups	Print the group membership of a user.
groupadd	Create a group.
groupdel	Delete a group.
groupmod	Modify a group.

A *group* is a set of accounts treated as a single entity. If you give permission for a group to take some action (such as modify a file), then all members of that group can take it. For example, you can give full permissions for the group **friends** to read, write, and execute the file */tmp/sample*:

```
$ groups
users smith friends
$ chgrp friends /tmp/sample
$ chmod 770 /tmp/sample
$ ls -l /tmp/sample
-rwxrwx--- 1 smith friends  2874 Oct 20 22:35 /tmp/sample
```

To add users to a group, edit */etc/group* as root.[18] To change the group ownership of a file, recall the **chgrp** commands from "File Properties" on page 59.

---

18. Different systems may store the group member list in other ways.

groups

groups [*usernames*]

The groups command prints the Linux groups to which you belong, or to which other users belong:

```
$ whoami
smith
$ groups
smith users
$ groups jones root
jones : jones users
root : root bin daemon sys adm disk wheel src
```

groupadd

groupadd [*options*] *group*

The groupadd command creates a group. In most cases, you should use the -f option to prevent duplicate groups from being created:

```
# groupadd -f friends
```

Useful options

-g *gid*   Specify your own numeric group ID instead of letting groupadd choose one.

-f   If the specified group exists already, complain and exit.

groupdel

groupdel *group*

The groupdel command deletes an existing group.

```
# groupdel friends
```

Before doing this, it's a good idea to identify all files that have their group ID set to the given group, so you can deal with them later:

```
# find / -group friends -print
```

because groupdel does not change the group ownership of any files. It simply removes the group name from the system's records. If you

list such files, you'll see a numeric group ID in place of a group name.

---

groupmod stdin **stdout** - file **-- opt** --help --version

groupmod [*options*] *group*

The groupmod command modifies the given group, changing its name or group ID.

    # groupmod -n newname friends

groupmod does not affect any files owned by this group: it simply changes the ID or name in the system's records. Be careful when changing the ID, or these files will have group ownership by a non-existent group.

Useful options

-n *name*   Change the group's name to *name* (safe).

-g *gid*   Change the group's ID to *gid* (risky).

Host Information

uname	Print basic system information.
hostname	Print the system's hostname.
dnsdomain name	Same as hostname -d.
domainname	Same as hostname -y.
nisdomain name	Same as hostname -y.
ypdomainname	Same as hostname -y.
ip	Set and display network interface information.
ifconfig	Older command to set and display network interface information.

Every Linux machine (or *host*) has a name, a network IP address, and other properties. Here's how to display this information.

---

uname   stdin   **stdout**   - file   -- opt   --help   --version

uname [*options*]

The uname command prints fundamental information about your computer:

```
$ uname -a
Linux server.example.com 2.6.32-35-generic-pae #78-Ubuntu
  SMP Tue Oct 11 17:01:12 UTC 2011 i686 GNU/Linux
```

This includes the kernel name (Linux), hostname (server.example.com), kernel release (2.6.32-35-generic-pae), kernel version (#78-Ubuntu SMP Tue Oct 11 17:01:12 UTC 2011), hardware name (i686), processor type (i686), and operating system name (GNU/Linux). Each of these values can be printed individually using options.

Useful options

-a   All information.

-s   Only the kernel name (the default).

-n   Only the hostname, as with the hostname command.

-r   Only the kernel release.

-v   Only the kernel version.

-m   Only the hardware name.

-p   Only the processor type.

-i   Only the hardware platform.

-o   Only the operating system name.

hostname

hostname [*options*] [*name*]

The hostname command prints the name of your computer. Depending on how you have things set up, this might be the fully qualified hostname:

```
$ hostname
myhost.example.com
```

or your short hostname:

```
$ hostname
myhost
```

You can also set your hostname, as root:[19]

```
# hostname orange
```

However, hostnames and nameservers are complicated topics well beyond the scope of this book. Don't just blindly start setting hostnames!

Useful options

-i	Print your host's IP address.
-a	Print your host's alias name.
-s	Print your host's short name.
-f	Print your host's fully qualified name.
-d	Print your host's DNS domain name.
-y	Print your host's NIS or YP domain name.
-F *hostfile*	Set your hostname by reading the name from file *hostfile*.

---

ip

ip [*options*] *object command*...

---

19. This change might not survive a reboot. Some Linux distros require additional steps, such as placing the hostname into a configuration file that is read at boot time. Consult the documentation for your distro.

The `ip` command displays and sets various aspects of your computer's network interface. This topic is beyond the scope of the book, but we'll teach you a few tricks.

You can get information about the default network interface (usually called *eth0*):

```
$ ip addr show eth0
2: eth0: <BROADCAST,MULTICAST,UP,LOWER_UP> mtu 1500 ...
    link/ether 00:50:ba:48:4f:ba brd ff:ff:ff:ff:ff:ff
    inet 192.168.0.21/24 brd 192.168.0.255 scope global eth0
    inet6 fe80::21e:8cff:fe53:41e4/64 scope link
      valid_lft forever preferred_lft forever
```

This includes your MAC address (00:50:ba:48:4f:ba), your IP address (192.168.0.21), and various other information. To view all loaded network interfaces, run:

```
$ ip addr show
```

Some other useful commands for displaying network information include:

ip help
> See usage information for all these commands

ip addr
> Display IP addresses of your network devices

ip maddr
> Display multicast addresses of your network devices

ip link
> Display attributes of your network devices

ip route
> Display your routing table

ip monitor
> Begin monitoring your network devices; type ^C to stop

Each of these commands has various options: add help on the end (e.g., `ip link help`) for usage. Additionally, `ip` can modify your network: configuring your network devices, managing routing tables and rules, creating tunnels, and more. It's part of a suite of tools called *iproute2*. You'll need networking experience to understand this complex command; see the ip manpage to get started, or visit *http://lartc.org*.

---

ifconfig   stdin **stdout** - file -- opt **--help** **--version**

ifconfig [*options*] *interface*

The ifconfig command is an ancestor of ip. It is still found on many Linux systems but is less powerful (some would call it obsolete). We'll cover a few simple commands here, but you should be using ip instead.

To display information about the default network interface (usually called *eth0*):

```
$ ifconfig eth0
eth0  Link encap:Ethernet  HWaddr 00:50:BA:48:4F:BA
      inet addr:192.168.0.10  Bcast:192.168.0.255 ...
      UP BROADCAST RUNNING MULTICAST  MTU:1500 ...
      RX packets:1955231 errors:0 dropped:0 overruns:0 ...
      TX packets:1314765 errors:0 dropped:0 overruns:0 ...
      collisions:0 txqueuelen:100
      ...
```

This includes your MAC address (00:50:BA:48:4F:BA), your IP address (192.168.0.21), your netmask (255.255.255.0), and various other information. To view all loaded network interfaces, run:

```
$ ifconfig -a
```

Host Location

host	Look up hostnames, IP addresses, and DNS info.
whois	Look up the registrants of Internet domains.
ping	Check if a remote host is reachable.
traceroute	View the network path to a remote host.

When dealing with remote computers, you might want to know more about them. Who owns them? What are the IP addresses? Where on the network are they located?

---

host [*options*] *name* [*server*]

The host command looks up the hostname or IP address of a remote machine by querying DNS.

```
$ host www.ubuntu.org
www.ubuntu.com has address 91.189.90.41
$ host 91.189.90.41
41.90.189.91.in-addr.arpa domain name pointer
 jujube.canonical.com.
```

It can also find out much more:

```
$ host -a www.ubuntu.org
Trying "www.ubuntu.org"
;; ->>HEADER<<- opcode: QUERY, status: NOERROR, id: 16652
;; flags: qr rd ra; QUERY: 1, ANSWER: 1, AUTHORITY: 0, ...

;; QUESTION SECTION:
;www.ubuntu.org.                        IN      ANY

;; ANSWER SECTION:
www.ubuntu.org.         60      IN      CNAME   ubuntu.org.
```

though a full discussion of this output is beyond the scope of this book. The final, optional "server" parameter specifies a particular nameserver for the query:

```
$ host www.ubuntu.org ns2.dondominio.com
Using domain server:
Name: ns2.dondominio.com
Address: 93.93.67.2#53
Aliases:

www.ubuntu.org is an alias for ubuntu.org.
ubuntu.org has address 147.83.195.55
ubuntu.org mail is handled by 10 mx2.upc.es.
ubuntu.org mail is handled by 10 mx1.upc.es.
```

To see all options, type host by itself.

Useful options

-a Display all available information.

-t   Choose the type of nameserver query: A, AXFR, CNAME, HINFO, KEY, MX, NS, PTR,
      SIG, SOA, and so on.

Here's an example of the -t option to locate MX records:

```
$ host -t MX redhat.com
redhat.com mail is handled by 5 mx1.redhat.com.
redhat.com mail is handled by 10 mx2.redhat.com.
```

If the host command doesn't do what you want, try dig, another powerful DNS lookup utility. You might also encounter the nslookup command, mostly obsolete but still found on some Linux and Unix systems.

---

whois   stdin   **stdout**   - file   **-- opt**   **--help**   **--version**

whois [*options*] *domain_name*

The whois command looks up the registration of an Internet domain:

```
$ whois linuxmint.com
...
Domain name:    LINUXMINT.COM
...
 Administrative Contact:
    Lefebvre, Clement
...
 Technical Contact:
    Hostmaster, Servage
...
Registrar of Record: TUCOWS, INC.
Record expires on 07-Jun-2012.
Record created on 07-Jun-2006.
...
```

plus a few screens full of legal disclaimers from the registrar.

Useful options

-h *registrar*   Perform the lookup at the given registrar's server. For example,
                 whois -h whois.networksolutions.com yahoo.com.

-p *port*   Query the given the TCP port instead of the default, 43 (the whois
                 service).

---

ping

ping [*options*] *host*

The ping command tells you if a remote host is reachable. It sends small packets (ICMP packets to be precise) to a remote host and waits for responses.

```
$ ping google.com
PING google.com (74.125.226.144) from 192.168.0.10 :
56(84) bytes of data.
64 bytes from www.google.com (74.125.226.144): icmp_seq=0
  ttl=49 time=32.390 msec
64 bytes from www.google.com (74.125.226.144): icmp_seq=1
  ttl=49 time=24.208 msec
^C
--- google.com ping statistics ---
2 packets transmitted, 2 packets received, 0% packet loss
round-trip min/avg/max/mdev = 24.208/28.299/32.390/4.091 ms
```

Useful options

-c *N*   Ping at most *N* times.

-i *N*   Wait *N* seconds (default 1) between pings.

-n   Print IP addresses in the output, rather than hostnames.

---

traceroute

traceroute [*options*] *host* [*packet_length*]

The traceroute command prints the network path from your local host to a remote host, and the time it takes for packets to traverse the path.

```
$ traceroute yahoo.com
 1 server.example.com (192.168.0.20) 1.397 ms ...
 2  10.221.16.1 (10.221.16.1) 15.397 ms ...
 3 gbr2-p10.cb1ma.ip.att.net (12.123.40.190) 4.952 ms ...
...
...
16 p6.www.dcn.yahoo.com (216.109.118.69)  * ...
```

Each host in the path is sent three "probes" and the return times are reported. If five seconds pass with no response, traceroute prints an asterisk. Also, `traceroute` may be blocked by firewalls or unable to proceed for various reasons, in which case it prints a symbol:

Symbol	Meaning
!F	Fragmentation needed.
!H	Host unreachable.
!N	Network unreachable.
!P	Protocol unreachable.
!S	Source route failed.
!X	Communication administratively prohibited.
!N	ICMP unreachable code N.

The default packet size is 40 bytes, but you can change this with the final, optional *packet_length* parameter (e.g., `traceroute myhost 120`).

Useful options

-n   Numeric mode: print IP addresses instead of hostnames.

-w N Change the timeout from five seconds to N seconds.

Network Connections

ssh   Securely log into a remote host, or run commands on it.

telnet   Log into a remote host (insecure!).

scp   Securely copy files to/from a remote host (batch).

sftp   Securely copy files to/from a remote host (interactive).

ftp   Copy files to/from a remote host (interactive, insecure!).

With Linux, it's easy to establish network connections from one machine to another for remote logins and file transfers. Just make sure you do it securely.

ssh [*options*] *host* [*command*]

The ssh (Secure Shell) program securely logs you into a remote machine where you already have an account:

    $ ssh remote.example.com

Alternatively, it can invoke a program on that remote machine without logging you in:

    $ ssh remote.example.com who

ssh encrypts all data that travels across its connection, including your username and password (which you'll need to access the remote machine). The SSH protocol also supports other ways to authenticate, such as public keys and host IDs. See man sshd for details.

Useful options

-l *user*	Specify your remote username; otherwise, ssh assumes your local username. You can also use the syntax *username@host*:
	$ ssh smith@server.example.com
-p *port*	Use a *port* number other than the default (22).
-t	Allocate a tty on the remote system; useful when trying to run a remote command with an interactive user interface, such as a text editor.
-v	Produce verbose output, useful for debugging.

---

telnet   stdin   **stdout**   - file   -- opt   --help   --version

telnet [*options*] *host* [*port*]

The telnet program logs you into a remote machine where you already have an account.

    $ telnet remote.example.com

Avoid telnet for remote logins: most implementations are insecure and send your password over the network in plain text for anyone to steal. Use ssh instead, which protects your password and data via encryption. There are two exceptions:

- In a Kerberos environment, using enhanced ("kerberized") telnet software on both the client and server side. See *http://web.mit.edu/kerberos/* for more information.

- Connecting to a remote port when you aren't sending any sensitive information at all. For example, to check for the presence of a web server (port 80) on a remote system:

```
$ telnet remote.example.com 80
Trying 192.168.55.21...
Connected to remote.example.com (192.168.55.21).
Escape character is '^]'.
xxx                Type some junk and press Enter
<HTML><HEAD>       Yep, it's a web server
<TITLE>400 Bad Request</TITLE>
</HEAD><BODY>
<H1>Bad Request</H1>
Your browser sent a request that
this server could not understand.<P>
</BODY></HTML>
Connection closed by foreign host.
```

To discourage you further from using telnet, we aren't even going to describe its options.

---

scp   stdin   **stdout**   - file   -- opt   **--help**   **--version**

scp *local_spec remote_spec*

The scp (secure copy) command copies files and directories from one computer to another in batch. (For an interactive user interface, see sftp.) It encrypts all communication between the two machines. As a simple example, scp can copy a local file to a remote machine:

```
$ scp myfile remote.example.com:newfile
```

recursively copy a directory to a remote machine:

```
$ scp -r mydir remote.example.com:
```

copy a remote file to your local machine:

```
$ scp remote.example.com:myfile .
```

or recursively copy a remote directory to your local machine:

```
$ scp -r remote.example.com:mydir .
```

To specify an alternate username on the remote system, use the *username@host* syntax:

```
$ scp myfile smith@remote.example.com:
```

Useful options

-p   Duplicate all file attributes (permissions, timestamps) when copying.

-r   Recursively copy a directory and its contents.

-v   Produce verbose output, useful for debugging.

---

sftp   stdin   stdout   - file   -- opt   --help   --version

sftp (*host username@host*)

The sftp program copies files interactively and securely between two computers. (As opposed to scp, which copies files in batch.) The user interface is much like that of ftp, but ftp is not secure.

```
$ sftp remote.example.com
Password: ********
sftp> cd MyFiles
sftp> ls
README
file1
file2
file3
sftp> get file2
Fetching /home/smith/MyFiles/file2 to file2
sftp> quit
```

If your username on the remote system is different from your local one, use the *username@host* argument:

```
$ sftp smith@remote.example.com
```

Command	Meaning
help	View a list of available commands.
ls	List the files in the current remote directory.
lls	List the files in the current local directory.
pwd	Print the remote working directory.
lpwd	Print the local working directory.

Command	Meaning
cd *dir*	Change your remote directory to be *dir*.
lcd *dir*	Change your local directory to be *dir*.
get *file1* [*file2*]	Copy remote *file1* to local machine, optionally renamed as *file2*.
put *file1* [*file2*]	Copy local *file1* to remote machine, optionally renamed as *file2*.
mget *file**	Copy multiple remote files to the local machine using wildcards * and ?.
mput *file**	Copy multiple local files to the remote machine using wildcards * and ?.
quit	Exit sftp.

---

ftp   stdin   stdout   - file   -- opt   --help   --version

ftp [*options*] *host*

The ftp (File Transfer Protocol) program copies files between computers, but not in a secure manner: your username and password travel over the network as plain text. Use sftp instead if your remote server supports it.

The same commands we listed for sftp also work for ftp. (However, the two programs support other, differing commands, too.)

Email

thunderbird	Graphical mail client.
evolution	Graphical mail client.
mutt	Text-based mail client.
mail	Minimal text-based mail client.
mailq	View the outgoing mail queue on your system.

Linux includes a number of mail readers, some graphical and some entirely text-based. We'll look at several with different

---

purposes and strengths. Other Linux mailers include kmail, alpine, and the RMAIL and vm applications built into emacs.

---

thunderbird

stdin   stdout   - file   -- opt   **--help**   **--version**

```
thunderbird
```

Thunderbird is one of the most popular graphical email programs, available not only for Linux but also Windows and Macintosh. The first time you run Thunderbird, you'll be guided through a series of dialogs to set up your mail account. Once this is complete, the main Thunderbird window presents you with common email operations:

Inbox	View your mail
Write	Compose a new mail message
Get Mail	Check for new messages on your mail server
Reply	Reply to a message, only to the sender
Reply All	Reply to a message, to all addresses in the To and CC lines
Forward	Forward a message to a third party

Thunderbird is highly configurable. You can customize the entire look and feel of the program (known as the "Theme"), install add-ons to provide new features, and more. See *http://www.getthunderbird.com* for details.

---

evolution

stdin   stdout   - file   -- opt   **--help**   **--version**

```
evolution
```

Evolution is another popular graphical email program. Run the command `evolution` from the shell to get started. As with Thunderbird, the first time you run Evolution, you'll be guided to set up your mail account. Once this is complete, the main Evolution window offers you common email commands by point-and-click:

Inbox	View your mail
New	Compose a new mail message

Send/Receive	Check for new messages on your mail server
Reply	Reply to a message, only to the sender
Reply To All	Reply to a message, to all addresses in the To and CC lines
Forward	Forward a message to a third party

There are many more features, so experiment, and see *http://projects .gnome.org/evolution* for more information.

---

mutt

mutt [*options*]

Mutt is a text-based mailer that runs in an ordinary terminal (or terminal window), so it can be used both locally (e.g., in an X terminal window) or remotely over an SSH connection. It is very powerful, with many commands and options. To invoke it, type:

    $ mutt

When the main screen appears, any messages in your mailbox are listed briefly, one per line, and the following commands are available:

Keystroke	Meaning
Up arrow	Move to the previous message.
Down arrow	Move to the next message.
PageUp	Scroll up one pageful of messages.
PageDown	Scroll down one pageful of messages.
Home	Move to the first message.
End	Move to the last message.
m	Compose a new mail message. This invokes your default text editor. After editing the message and exiting the editor, type y to send the message or q to postpone it.
r	Reply to current message. Works like m.
f	Forward the current message to a third party. Works like m.
i	View the contents of your mailbox.

Keystroke	Meaning
C	Copy the current message to another mailbox.
d	Delete the current message.

While writing a message, after you exit your text editor, the following commands are available:

Keystroke	Meaning
a	Attach a file (an attachment) to the message.
c	Set the CC list.
b	Set the BCC list.
e	Edit the message again.
r	Edit the Reply-To field.
s	Edit the subject line.
y	Send the message.
C	Copy the message to a file.
q	Postpone the message without sending it.

Additional commands are always available:

Keystroke	Meaning
?	See a list of all commands (press the SPACEBAR to scroll down, q to quit).
^G	Cancel the command in progress.
q	Quit.

The official Mutt site is *http://www.mutt.org*.

---

mail   stdin   stdout   - file   -- opt   --help   --version

mail [*options*] *recipient*

The mail program (equivalently, Mail)[20] is a quick, simple email client. Most people want a more powerful program for regular use, but for quick messages from the command line or in scripts, mail is really handy.

To send a quick message:

```
$ mail smith@example.com
Subject: my subject
I'm typing a message.
To end it, I type a period by itself on a line.


.
Cc: jones@example.com
$
```

To send a quick message using a single command, use a pipeline:

```
$ echo "Hello world" | mail -s "subject" smith@example.com
```

To mail a file using a single command, you can use redirection or a pipeline:

```
$ mail -s "my subject" smith@example.com < filename
$ cat filename | mail -s "my subject" smith@example.com
```

Notice how easily you can send the output of a pipeline as an email message; this is useful in scripts.

Useful options

-s *subject*	Set the subject line of an outgoing message.
-v	Verbose mode: print messages about mail delivery.
-c *addresses*	CC the message to the given addresses, a comma-separated list.
-b *addresses*	BCC the message to the given addresses, a comma-separated list.

---

mailq   stdin **stdout** - file -- opt --help --version

mailq

The mailq command lists any outgoing email messages awaiting delivery.

---

20. On older Unix systems, Mail and mail were rather different programs, but on Linux they are the same: */usr/bin/Mail* is a symbolic link to the mail command.

```
$ mailq
Queue ID- --Size-- ----Arrival Time-- -Sender/Recipient---
46AAB43972*    333 Tue Jan 10 21:17:14 smith@example.com
                                        jones@elsewhere.org
```

Sent mail messages are also recorded in a log file such as */var/log/maillog*; the name may differ from distro to distro.

Beyond Mail Readers

Email is more "transparent" on Linux than on other platforms that merely display your mailbox and send and receive messages. The ability to list outgoing email messages with mailq is just one example. Here are some other options to whet your appetite and encourage you to explore.

- You can process your mailboxes with any command-line tools, such as grep, because mail files are plain text.

- You can manually retrieve messages from your mail server at the command line with the fetchmail command. Using a simple configuration file, this command can reach out to IMAP and POP servers and download mail in batch. See man fetch mail.

- Your system can run a mail server, such as postfix or send mail, to handle the most complex mail delivery situations.

- You can control local mail delivery in sophisticated ways with the procmail command, which filters arriving email messages through any arbitrary program. See man procmail.

- Spam filtering is sophisticated on Linux: check out the SpamAssassin suite of programs. You can run it personally on your incoming email, or at the server level for large numbers of users.

In short, email is not limited to the features of your mail-reading program. Investigate and experiment!

Web Browsing

`firefox`	Full-featured web browser.
`lynx`	Text-only web browser.
`wget`	Download web pages and files.

Linux offers several ways to explore the World Wide Web: traditional browsers, text-based browsers, and page-retrieval utilities.

---

firefox
stdin   stdout   - file   -- opt   **--help**   **--version**

`firefox [options] [URL]`

Firefox is one of the most popular web browsers for Linux and most other operating systems. Start it in the background with:

```
$ firefox &
```

Some other web browsers for Linux include Google Chrome (*http://www.google.com/chrome*), Opera (*http://www.opera.com*), Konqueror for KDE (*http://www.konqueror.org*), and Epiphany for GNOME (*http://projects.gnome.org/epiphany*).

---

lynx
stdin   **stdout**   - file   -- opt   **--help**   **--version**

`lynx [options] [URL]`

Lynx is a stripped-down, text-only web browser. It doesn't display pictures, play audio or video, or even respond to your mouse. But it's incredibly useful when you just want a quick look at a page, or when the network is slow, or for downloading the HTML of a website. It's particularly good for checking out a suspicious URL, since Lynx doesn't run JavaScript and won't even accept a cookie without asking you first.

```
$ lynx http://www.yahoo.com
```

All browsing is done by keyboard. Many pages will not look quite right, especially if they use tables or frames extensively, but usually you can find your way around a site.

Keystroke	Meaning
?	Get help.
k	List all keystrokes and their meanings.
^G	Cancel a command in progress.
q	Quit Lynx.
Enter	"Click" the current link, or finish the current form field.
Left arrow	Back to previous page.
Right arrow	Forward to next page, or "click" the current link.
g	Go to a URL (you'll be prompted to enter it).
p	Save, print, or mail the current page.
Space bar	Scroll down.
b	Scroll up.
Down arrow	Go to the next link or form field.
Up arrow	Go to the previous link or form field.
^A	Go to top of page.
^E	Go to end of page.
m	Return to the main/home page.
/	Search for text on the page.
a	Bookmark the current page.
v	View your bookmark list.
r	Delete a bookmark.
=	Display properties of the current page and link.
\	View HTML source (type again to return to normal view).

Lynx has over 100 command-line options, so the manpage is well worth exploring.

Useful options

-dump	Print the rendered page to standard output and exit. (Compare to the -source option.)
-source	Print the HTML source to standard output and exit. (Compare to the wget command.)
-emacskeys	Make Lynx obey keystrokes reminiscent of the emacs editor.
-vikeys	Make Lynx obey keystrokes reminiscent of the vim (or vi) editor.
-homepage=URL	Set your home page URL to be URL.
-color	Turn colored text mode on.
-nocolor	Turn colored text mode off.

---

wget   stdin   stdout   - file   -- opt   --help   --version

wget [*options*] *URL*

The wget command hits a URL and downloads the data to a file or standard output. It's great for capturing individual web pages, downloading files, or duplicating entire web site hierarchies to arbitrary depth. For example, let's capture the Yahoo home page:

```
$ wget http://www.yahoo.com
23:19:51 (220.84 KB/s) - `index.html' saved [31434]
```

which is saved to a file *index.html* in the current directory. wget has the added ability to resume a download if it gets interrupted in the middle, say, due to a network failure: just run wget -c with the same URL and it picks up where it left off.

Perhaps the most useful feature of wget is its ability to download files without needing a web browser:

```
$ wget http://www.example.com/files/manual.pdf
```

This is great for large files like videos and ISO images. You can even write shell scripts to download sets of files if you know their names:

```
$ for i in 1 2 3; do wget http://example.com/$i.mpeg; done
```

Another similar command is curl, which writes to standard output by default—unlike wget, which duplicates the original page and file names by default.

```
$ curl http://www.yahoo.com > mypage.html
```

wget has over 70 options, so we'll cover just a few important ones.
(curl has a different set of options; see its manpage.)

Useful options

-i *filename*	Read URLs from the given file and retrieve them in turn.
-O *filename*	Write all the captured HTML to the given file, one page appended after the other.
-c	Continue mode: if a previous retrieval was interrupted, leaving only a partial file as a result, pick up where wget left off. That is, if wget had downloaded 100K of a 150K file, the -c option says to retrieve only the remaining 50K and append it to the existing file. wget can be fooled, however, if the remote file has changed since the first (partial) download, so use this option only if you know the remote file hasn't changed.
-t *N*	Try *N* times before giving up. *N* = 0 means try forever.
--progress=dot	Print dots to show the download progress.
--progress=bar	Print bars to show the download progress.
--spider	Don't download, just check existence of remote pages.
-nd	Retrieve all files into the current directory, even if remotely they are in a more complex directory tree. (By default, wget duplicates the remote directory hierarchy.)
-r	Retrieve a page hierarchy recursively, including subdirectories.
-l *N*	Retrieve files at most *N* levels deep (5 by default).
-k	Inside retrieved files, modify URLs so the files can be viewed locally in a web browser.
-p	Download all necessary files to make a page display completely, such as stylesheets and images.
-L	Follow relative links (within a page) but not absolute links.
-A *pattern*	Accept mode: download only files whose names match a given pattern. Patterns may contain the same wildcards as the shell.

-R *pattern*	Reject mode: download only files whose names *do not* match a given pattern.
-I *pattern*	Directory inclusion: download files only from directories that match a given pattern.
-X *pattern*	Directory exclusion: download files only from directories that *do not* match a given pattern.

Usenet News

Usenet News is one of the oldest communities online today. It consists of tens of thousands of *newsgroups*, discussion forums in which people post (submit) messages and reply to them. One common, text-based newsreader program is slrn, but there are dozens more available on the Net (rn, trn, tin, and so on). Usenet News can also be searched at Google Groups, *http:// groups.google.com*.

In order to access Usenet, you need to connect to a news server, an Internet host that permits reading and posting of news articles. Once you can connect to a news server (say, *news.example.com*), a record of your subscribed newsgroups and which articles you've read is kept in a file in your home directory automatically. Depending on your newsreader configuration, the file is either ~/.newsrc or ~/.jnewsrc.

---

slrn   stdin   **stdout**   - file   -- opt   --help   --version

slrn [*options*]

slrn is a Usenet newsreader. Before using it, you must specify a news server by setting your shell's NNTPSERVER variable:

```
$ export NNTPSERVER=news.example.com
```

Then create a newsgroups file (only if you haven't used slrn on this computer before):

```
$ slrn --create
```

---

and start reading news:

```
$ slrn
```

When invoked, `slrn` displays the News Groups page with a list of your subscribed newsgroups. Some useful commands are:

Keystroke	Meaning
q	Quit `slrn`.
Down	Select next newsgroup.
Up	Select previous newsgroup.
Enter	Read the selected newsgroup.
p	Post a new article in the selected newsgroup.
a	Add a new newsgroup (you must know the name).
u	Unsubscribe from the selected newsgroup (it will be removed after you quit). Type s to resubscribe.

When you press Enter to read a newsgroup, `slrn` displays a Group page, containing the available discussions (or "threads") in that newsgroup. Some useful commands on this page are:

Keystroke	Meaning
q	Quit and go back to the News Groups page.
Down	Select next thread.
Up	Select previous thread.
Enter	Begin reading the selected thread.
c	Mark all threads as read ("catch up"): type ESCAPE u to undo.

Commands while reading an article include:

Keystroke	Meaning
q	Quit reading and return to the Group page.
Space bar	Go to next page of article.
b	Go back to previous page of article.
r	Reply to the author by email.
f	Post a followup article.

Keystroke	Meaning
P	Post a new article.
o	Save the article in a file.
n	Go to next unread article.
p	Go to previous unread article.

At any time you can type ? for the help page. slrn has a tremendous number of commands and options, and can be configured via the file *~/.slrnrc*. We've covered only the basics; see */usr/share/doc/slrn** and www.slrn.org for more information.

Instant Messaging

pidgin	Instant messaging and IRC client.
talk	Linux/Unix chat program.
write	Send messages to a terminal.
mesg	Prohibit talk and write.
tty	Print your terminal device name.

Linux provides various ways to send messages to other users on the same machine or elsewhere on the Internet. These range from the ancient programs talk and write, which work over Linux terminal devices (ttys), to more modern instant messaging clients like pidgin.

---

pidgin   stdin   stdout   - file   -- opt   **--help**   **--version**

pidgin [*options*]

pidgin is a instant messaging client that works with many different protocols, including AOL, MSN, Yahoo, and more. It is also an IRC (Internet Relay Chat) client. It runs in an X window:

```
$ pidgin &
```

If you don't already have an account with one of these IM services, you'll need to create one first; for example, visit www.aim.com to create an AOL Instant Messenger account. Once this is done, simply click the Accounts button to indicate your account to pidgin, enter your screen name and password in the login window, and you should be connected.

Useful options

-l *accounts*	Enable the given accounts (a comma-separated list).
-n	Don't automatically log in when invoking pidgin (assuming your password is stored).
-m	Let multiple copies of pidgin run at the same time.

---

talk   stdin   stdout   - file   -- opt   --help   --version

talk [*user*[@*host*]] [*tty*]

The talk program predates modern instant messaging by a few decades: it connects two users, logged in on the same or different hosts, for one-to-one communication. It runs in a shell window, splitting it horizontally, so you can see your own typing and that of your partner.

```
$ talk friend@example.com
```

If your partner is logged in multiple times, you can specify one of his ttys for the talk connection.

---

write   stdin   stdout   - file   -- opt   --help   --version

write *user* [*tty*]

The write program is more primitive than talk: it sends lines of text from one logged-in user to another on the same Linux machine.

```
$ write smith
Hi, how are you?
See you later.
^D
```

^D ends the connection. write is also useful in pipelines for quick one-off messages:

```
$ echo 'Howdy!' | write smith
```

---

mesg   stdin   stdout   - file   -- opt   --help   --version

mesg [y|n]

The mesg program controls whether talk and write connections can reach your terminal. mesg y permits them, mesg n denies them, and mesg prints the current status (y or n). The default is y. mesg has no effect on modern instant messaging programs like pidgin.

```
$ mesg
is y
$ mesg n
$ mesg
is n
```

---

tty   stdin   stdout   - file   -- opt   **--help**   **--version**

tty

The tty program prints the name of the terminal device associated with the current shell.

```
$ tty
/dev/pts/4
```

Screen Output

echo	Print simple text on standard output.
printf	Print formatted text on standard output.
yes	Print repeated text on standard output.
seq	Print a sequence of numbers on standard output.
clear	Clear the screen or window.

Linux provides several commands for printing messages on standard output:

```
$ echo hello world
hello world
```

Each command has different strengths and intended purposes. These commands are invaluable for learning about Linux, debugging problems, writing shell scripts (see "Programming with Shell Scripts" on page 195), or just talking to yourself.

---

echo

echo [*options*] *strings*

The echo command simply prints its arguments:

```
$ echo We are having fun
We are having fun
```

Unfortunately, there are several different echo commands with slightly different behavior. There's */bin/echo*, but Linux shells typically override this with a built-in command called echo. To find out which you're using, run the command type echo.

Useful options

-n   Don't print a final newline character.

-e   Recognize and interpret escape characters. For example, try echo 'hello\a' and echo -e 'hello\a'. The first prints literally and the second makes a beep.

-E   Don't interpret escape characters: the opposite of -e.

Available escape characters are:

\a   Alert (play a beep)

\b   Backspace

\c   Don't print the final newline (same effect as -n)

\f   Form feed

\n   Line feed (newline)

\r   Carriage return

\t	Horizontal tab
\v	Vertical tab
\\	A backslash
\'	Single quote
\"	Double quote
\nnn	The character whose ASCII value is nnn in octal

---

printf   stdin **stdout** - file **-- opt** --help --version

printf *format_string* [*arguments*]

The printf command is an enhanced echo: it prints formatted strings on standard output. It operates much like the C programming language function printf( ), which applies a format string to a sequence of arguments to create some specified output. For example:

```
$ printf "User %s is %d years old.\n" sandy 29
User sandy is 29 years old.
```

The first argument is the format string, which in our example contains two format specifications, %s and %d. The subsequent arguments, sandy and 29, are substituted by printf into the format string and then printed. Format specifications can get fancy with floating-point numbers:

```
$ printf "That\'ll be $%0.2f, sir.\n" 3
That'll be $3.00, sir.
```

There are two printf commands available in Linux: one built into the bash shell, and one in */usr/bin/printf*. The two are identical except for one format specification, %q, supported only by the bash built-in: it prints escape symbols ("\") so its output can be used as shell input safely. Note the difference:

```
$ printf "This is a quote: %s\n" "\""
This is a quote: "
$ printf "This is a quote: %q\n" "\""
This is a quote: \"
```

It is your responsibility to make sure the number of format specifications (%) equals the number of arguments supplied to printf. If

---

you have too many arguments, the extras are ignored, and if you have too few, printf assumes default values (0 for numeric formats, an empty string for string formats). Nevertheless, you should treat such mismatches as errors, even though printf is forgiving. If they lurk in your shell scripts, they are bugs waiting to happen.

Format specifications are described in detail on the manpage for the C function printf (see man 3 printf). Here are some useful ones.

%d	Decimal integer
%ld	Long decimal integer
%o	Octal integer
%x	Hexadecimal integer
%f	Floating point
%lf	Double-precision floating point
%c	A single character
%s	String
%q	String with any shell metacharacters escaped
%%	A percent sign by itself

Just after the leading percent sign, you can insert a numeric expression for the minimum width of the output. For example, "%5d" means to print a decimal number in a five-character-wide field, and "%6.2f" means a floating-point number in a six-character-wide field with two digits after the decimal point. Some useful numeric expressions are:

n	Minimum width n.
0n	Minimum width n, padded with leading zeroes.
$n.m$	Minimum width n, with m digits after the decimal point.

printf also interprets escape characters like "\n" (print a newline character) and "\a" (ring the bell). See the echo command for the full list.

yes   stdin **stdout** - file -- opt **--help** **--version**

yes [*string*]

The yes command prints the given string (or "y" by default) forever, one string per line.

```
$ yes again
again
again
again
...
```

Though it might seem useless at first glance, yes can be perfect for turning interactive commands into batch commands. Want to get rid of an annoying "Are you SURE you want to do that?" message? Pipe the output of yes into the input of the command to answer all those prompts:

```
$ yes | my_interactive_command
```

When *my_interactive_command* terminates, so will yes.

---

seq   stdin **stdout** - file -- opt **--help** **--version**

seq [*options*] *specification*

The seq command prints a sequence of integers or real numbers, suitable for piping to other programs. There are three kinds of specification arguments:

A single number: an upper limit
    seq begins at 1 and counts up to the number.

```
$ seq 3
1
2
3
```

Two numbers: lower and upper limit
    seq begins at the first number and counts as far as it can without passing the second number.

```
$ seq 2 5
2
3
```

```
4
5
```

Three numbers: lower limit, increment, and upper limit

seq begins at the first number, increments by the second number, and stops at (or before) the third number.

```
$ seq 1 .3 2
1
1.3
1.6
1.9
```

You can also go backward with a negative increment:

```
$ seq 5 -1 2
5
4
3
2
```

Useful options

-w   Print leading zeroes, as necessary, to give all lines the same width:

```
$ seq -w 8 10
08
09
10
```

-f *format*   Format the output lines with a printf-like format string, which must include either %g (the default), %e, or %f:

```
$ seq -f '**%g**' 3
**1**
**2**
**3**
```

-s *string* Use the given string as a separator between the numbers. By default, a newline is printed (i.e., one number per line):

```
$ seq -s ':' 10
1:2:3:4:5:6:7:8:9:10
```

clear   stdin   **stdout**   - file   -- opt   --help   --version

```
clear
```

This command simply clears your display or shell window.

Math and Calculations

xcalc   Display a graphical calculator.

expr   Evaluate simple math on the command line.

dc   Text-based calculator.

Need a calculator? Linux provides not only a familiar graphical calculator, but also some command-line programs to compute mathematical truths for you.

---

xcalc   stdin   stdout   - file   -- opt   --help   --version

```
xcalc [options]
```

The xcalc command displays a simple, graphical calculator in an X window. The default is a traditional calculator; if you prefer a reverse-polish notation (RPN) calculator, supply the -rpn option.

---

expr   stdin   **stdout**   - file   -- opt   **--help**   **--version**

```
expr expression
```

The expr command does simple math (and other expression evaluation) on the command line:

```
$ expr 7 + 3
10
$ expr '(' 7 + 3 ')' '*' 14      Special shell characters are quoted
140
$ expr length ABCDEFG
7
$ expr 15 '>' 16
0                                Meaning false
```

Each argument must be separated by whitespace. Notice that we had to quote or escape any characters that have special meaning to the shell. Parentheses (escaped) may be used for grouping. Operators for expr include:

Operator	Numeric operation	String operation
+	Addition	
-	Subtraction	
*	Multiplication	
/	Integer division	
%	Remainder (modulo)	
<	Less than	Earlier in dictionary.
<=	Less than or equal	Earlier in dictionary, or equal.
>	Greater than	Later in dictionary.
>=	Greater than or equal	Later in dictionary, or equal.
=	Equality	Equality.
!=	Inequality	Inequality.
		Boolean "or"	Boolean "or".
&	Boolean "and"	Boolean "and".
s : regexp		Does the regular expression regexp match string s?
substr s p n		Print n characters of string s, beginning at position p. (p=1 is the first character.)
index s chars		Return the index of the first position in string s containing a character from string chars. Return 0 if not found. Same behavior as the C function index( ).

For Boolean expressions, the number 0 and the empty string are considered false; any other value is true. For Boolean results, 0 is false and 1 is true.

expr is not very efficient. For more complex needs, consider using a language like Perl instead.

---

dc

stdin   stdout   - file   -- opt   --help   --version

dc [*options*] [*files*]

The **dc** (desk calculator) command is a reverse-polish notation (RPN), stack-based calculator that reads expressions from standard input and writes results to standard output. If you know how to use a Hewlett-Packard RPN calculator, **dc** is pretty easy to use once you understand its syntax. But if you're used to traditional calculators, **dc** may seem inscrutable. We'll cover only some basic commands.

For stack and calculator operations:

q	Quit **dc**.
f	Print the entire stack.
c	Delete (clear) the entire stack.
p	Print the topmost value on the stack.
P	Pop (remove) the topmost value from the stack.
n k	Set precision of future operations to be *n* decimal places (default is 0: integer operations).

To pop the top two values from the stack, perform a requested operation, and push the result:

+	Addition.
-	Subtraction.
*	Multiplication.
/	Division.
%	Remainder.
^	Exponentiation (second-to-top value is the base, top value is the exponent).

To pop the top value from the stack, perform a requested operation, and push the result:

v   Square root.

Examples:

```
$ dc
4 5 + p          Print the sum of 4 and 5
9
2 3 ^ p          Raise 2 to the 3rd power and print the result
8
10 * p           Multiply the stack top by 10 and print the result
80
f                Print the stack
80
9
+p               Pop the top two stack values and print their sum
89
```

Dates and Times

xclock   Display a graphical clock.

cal   Print a calendar.

date   Print or set the date and time.

ntpdate   Set the system time using a remote timeserver.

Need a date? How about a good time? Try these programs to display and set dates and times on your system.

---

xclock   stdin   stdout - file -- opt --help --version

xclock [*options*]

The xclock command displays a simple, graphical clock in an X window. If you prefer a different style, there are other clock programs included, such as oclock (round clock) and the taskbar clocks displayed by GNOME and KDE.

Useful options

`-analog`	An analog clock with hands.
`-digital [-brief]`	A digital clock with full date and time; add `-brief` to show only the time.
`-update N`	Update the time display every *N* seconds.

---

cal

stdin   **stdout**   - file   -- opt   --help   --version

`cal [options] [month [year]]`

The `cal` command prints a calendar—by default, the current month:

```
$ cal
    December 2011
Su Mo Tu We Th Fr Sa
             1  2  3
 4  5  6  7  8  9 10
11 12 13 14 15 16 17
18 19 20 21 22 23 24
25 26 27 28 29 30 31
```

To print a different calendar, supply a month and four-digit year: `cal 8 2011`. If you omit the month (`cal 2011`), the entire year is printed.

Useful options

- `-y`   Print the current year's calendar.

- `-3`   Three-month view: print the previous and next month as well.

- `-j`   Number each day by its position in the year; in our example, September 1 would be displayed as 244, September 2 as 245, and so on.

---

date

stdin   **stdout**   - file   -- opt   **--help**   **--version**

`date [options] [format]`

The `date` command prints dates and times. The results will depend on your system's locale settings (for your country and language). In this section we assume an English, US-based locale.

By default, date prints the system date and time in the local time-zone:

```
$ date
Sun Sep 28 21:01:31 EDT 2003
```

You can format the output differently by supplying a format string beginning with a plus sign:

```
$ date '+%D'
09/28/03
$ date '+The time is %l:%M %p on a beautiful %A in %B'
The time is  9:01 PM on a beautiful Sunday in September
```

Here is a sampling of the date command's many formats:

Format	Meaning	Example (US English)
Whole dates and times:		
%c	Full date and time, 12-hour clock	Sun 28 Sep 2003, 09:01:25 PM EDT
%D	Numeric date, 2-digit year	09/28/03
%x	Numeric date, 4-digit year	09/28/2003
%T	Time, 24-hour clock	21:01:25
%X	Time, 12-hour clock	09:01:25 PM
Words:		
%a	Day of week (abbreviated)	Sun
%A	Day of week (complete)	Sunday
%b	Month name (abbreviated)	Sep
%B	Month name (complete)	September
%Z	Time zone	EDT
%p	AM or PM	PM
Numbers:		
%w	Day of week (0–6, 0=Sunday)	0
%u	Day of week (1–7, 1=Monday)	7
%d	Day of month, leading zero	02
%e	Day of month, leading blank	2
%j	Day of year, leading zeroes	005

Format	Meaning	Example (US English)
%m	Month number, leading zero	09
%y	Year, 2 digits	03
%Y	Year, 4 digits	2003
%M	Minute, leading zero	09
%S	Seconds, leading zero	05
%l	Hour, 12-hour clock, leading blank	9
%I	Hour, 12-hour clock, leading zero	09
%k	Hour, 24-hour clock, leading blank	9
%H	Hour, 24-hour clock, leading zero	09
%N	Nanoseconds	737418000
%s	Seconds since the beginning of Linux time: midnight January 1, 1970	1068583983

Other:

%n	Newline character	
%t	Tab character	
%%	Percent sign	%

Through its options, date can also display other dates and times.

Useful options

-d *date_or_time_string*	Display the given *date_or_time_string*, formatted as you wish.
-r *filename*	Display the last-modified timestamp of the given file, formatted as you wish.
-s *date_or_time_string*	Set the system date and/or time; only the superuser can do this.

ntpdate

stdin   **stdout**   - file   **-- opt**   --help   --version

ntpdate *timeserver*

The ntpdate command sets the current system time by contacting a timeserver machine on the network. You must be root to set the system time.

```
# /usr/sbin/ntpdate timeserver.someplace.edu
  7 Sep 21:01:25 ntpdate[2399]: step time server 178.99.1.8
    offset 0.51 sec
```

To keep your system date in sync with a timeserver over long periods, use the daemon ntpd instead; see *http://www.ntp.org*. If you don't know a local timeserver, search Google for "public ntp time server".

Graphics and Screensavers

eog	Display graphics files.
geeqie	Display graphics files and slideshows.
ksnapshot	Take a screenshot (screen capture).
gimp	Edit graphics files.
dia	Draw structured diagrams.
gnuplot	Create graphs and plots.
xscreensaver	Run a screensaver.

For viewing or editing graphics, Linux has handy tools with tons of options. We won't cover these programs in much detail, just enough to pique your interest. Our goal is to make you aware of the programs so you can explore further on your own.

---

eog   stdin   stdout   - file   -- opt   **--help**   **--version**

eog [*options*] [*files*]

The eog (Eye of Gnome) image viewer displays graphics files in a variety of formats. If you invoke it for a single file, it displays the file. Invoked on two or more files:

```
$ eog file1.jpg file2.gif file3.pbm
```

it displays each in a separate window.

Useful options

-f   Display images in full-screen mode.

-s   Display images in a slideshow.

geeqie   stdin   stdout   - file   -- opt   **--help**   **--version**

geeqie [*options*] [*file*]

The geeqie image viewer (the successor to gqview) displays graphics files in a variety of formats, and can automatically switch from one image to the next, like a slideshow. By default, it displays the names of all graphics files in the current directory, and you can select names to display the images. The onscreen menus are straightforward, so explore them and try things out. Type ^q to quit.

Useful options

-f   Display images in full-screen mode. (Toggle between full-screen mode and window mode by typing v.)

-s   Display images in a slideshow. (Turn the slideshow on and off by typing s.)

ksnapshot   stdin   stdout   - file   -- opt   **--help**   **--version**

ksnapshot [*options*]

The ksnapshot command is a versatile screen-capture utility. Simply run:

    $ ksnapshot

and it takes a screenshot, displaying it in miniature. From there you can save it to a graphics file or take another screenshot. The file format will match whatever file extension you choose: *.jpg* to produce a JPEG file, *.bmp* for a Windows bitmap, *.pbm* for a portable bitmap, *.eps* for encapsulated PostScript, *.ico* for a Windows icon, and so forth. For a list of supported file formats, click the Save Snapshot button and view the selections under Filter. For more information, click the Help button in the ksnapshot window, or run ksnapshot --help-all from the shell.

---

gimp

gimp [*options*] [*files*]

The GIMP (GNU Image Manipulation Program) is a full-featured image-editing package that rivals Adobe Photoshop in power and scope. It is fairly complex to use, but the results can be stunning. Visit *http://www.gimp.org* for full information. To run the program, type:

    $ gimp

To edit a particular file, type:

    $ gimp *filename*

If the GIMP is more complicated than you need, try Pinta (*http:// pinta-project.com/*) or xv (*http://www.trilon.com/xv*). xv is no longer maintained, but it's one of this author's favorite utilities:

    $ xv myfile.jpg

Click the right mouse button anywhere on the image to reveal the menu of editing tools.

---

dia

dia [*options*] [*files*]

The dia program creates structured drawings such as flowcharts, schematics, entity-relation (ER) diagrams, and more. It's like a mini Microsoft Visio. Diagrams can be exported in popular formats like JPEG, PDF, and PNG. See *http://live.gnome.org/Dia* for full details.

---

gnuplot

gnuplot [*options*] [*files*]

The gnuplot program creates graphs, plotting points and connecting them with lines and curves, and saves them in a wide variety of printer and plotter formats, such as PostScript. To use gnuplot, you need to learn a small but powerful programming language. Here's an example of plotting the curve $y = x^2$ from $x = 1$ to 10, which will appear in an X window on your display:

```
$ gnuplot
gnuplot> plot [1:10] x**2
gnuplot> quit
```

To do the same, saving the results as a PostScript file:

```
$ cat myfile
set terminal postscript
plot [1:10] x**2
$ gnuplot < myfile > output.ps
```

See *http://www.gnuplot.info* for full details.

---

xscreensaver   stdin   stdout   - file   -- opt   **--help**   --version

xscreensaver

The xscreensaver system is a versatile screen saver with hundreds
of animations available. KDE and GNOME have their own screensavers and options, but if you prefer, you can run xscreensaver
manually.

xscreensaver runs in the background, and you can control it in various ways:

After a period of inactivity.
> You can configure xscreensaver to run automatically after a
> period of inactivity, such as five minutes.

As a screen locker.
> xscreensaver can also lock your screen on request. Your dis-
> play will remain locked until you enter your login password.

On the command line.
> Run xscreensaver-demo to preview the many animations and
> set things up the way you like. Then run xscreensaver-com
> mand to control the program's behavior:

```
$ xscreensaver-command -activate    Blank now
$ xscreensaver-command -next        Choose next animation
$ xscreensaver-command -prev        Choose previous animation
$ xscreensaver-command -cycle       Choose random animation
$ xscreensaver-command -lock        Lock the screen now
$ xscreensaver-command -exit        Quit
```

Audio

amarok	Audio file player (MP3, WAV, OGG).
grip	CD player, ripper, and MP3 encoder.
cdparanoia	Rip audio from CDs to WAV files.
lame	Convert from WAV to MP3.
id3tag	Edit ID3 tags.
audacity	Edit audio files.
k3b	CD burner with graphical interface.

Audio is alive and well on Linux systems. Most of the programs we'll cover have intuitive user interfaces, tons of features, and reasonable documentation, so we won't discuss them in detail. Mainly, we want you to have a taste of what's available and possible. Visit *http://linux-sound.org/* for a directory of Linux audio and MIDI programs.

---

amarok   stdin   stdout   - file   -- opt   **--help**   **--version**

xmms [*options*] [*files or URLs*]

Linux has numerous audio file players, including amarok, audacious, rhythmbox, and more. We'll cover amarok, but your system probably has several of these programs installed.

The easiest way to get started with amarok is to try it, either with no arguments:

```
$ amarok
```

or providing audio files or URLs on the command line:

```
$ amarok file1.mp3 file2.wav file3.ogg ...
$ amarok http://www.example.com/song.mp3
```

Useful options

--pause	Pause the current track.
--play	Begin playing.

`--stop`	Stop playing.
`--previous`	Play the previous track.
`--next`	Play the next track.

grip

stdin   stdout   - file   -- opt   --help   --version

`grip [options]`

grip is a CD player and an audio ripper: it can play CDs, extract audio from CDs, save it in WAV files, and convert the files to MP3s. It has extensive built-in help and fairly intuitive controls.

grip hasn't been updated in quite a while (though it's very good), so if you prefer a program that's still maintained, check out Sound Juicer (*http://burtonini.com/blog/computers/sound-juicer/*) or KAudioCreator (*http://www.kde.org/applications/multimedia/kaudiocreator/*).

cdparanoia

stdin   stdout   - file   -- opt   --help   --version

`cdparanoia [options] span [outfile]`

The **cdparanoia** command reads (rips) audio data from a CD and stores it in WAV files (or other formats: see the manpage). Common uses are:

`$ cdparanoia N`
> Rip track *N* to a file.

`$ cdparanoia -B`
> Rip all tracks on the CD into separate files.

`$ cdparanoia -B 2-4`
> Rip tracks 2, 3, and 4 into separate files.

`$ cdparanoia 2-4`
> Rip tracks 2, 3, and 4 into a single file.

If you have difficulty accessing your drive, try running **cdparanoia** `-Qvs` ("search for CD-ROM drives verbosely") and look for clues.

lame

stdin   stdout   - **file**   – opt   **--help**   **--version**

lame [*options*] *file*.wav

The lame command converts a WAV audio file (say, *song.wav*) into an MP3 file:

```
$ lame song.wav song.mp3
```

It has over 100 options to control bit rate, convert other formats, add ID3 tags, and much more.

id3tag

stdin   stdout   - **file**   -- opt   **--help**   **--version**

id3tag [*options*] *files*

The id3tag command adds or modifies ID3 tags in an MP3 file. For example, to tag an MP3 file with a new title and artist, run:

```
$ id3tag -A "My Album" -a "Loud Linux Squad" song.mp3
```

Useful options

-A *name*	Set the artist's name
-a *title*	Set the album title
-s *title*	Set the song title
-y *year*	Set the year
-t *number*	Set the track number
-g *number*	Set the genre number

audacity

stdin   stdout   - file   -- opt   --help   --version

audacity [*files*]

audacity is a graphical audio file editor for making changes to WAV, MP3, and Ogg files. Once a file is loaded, you can view its waveform, cut and paste audio data, apply filters and special effects to the sound (echo, bass boost, reverse, etc.), and more. See *http://audacity.sourceforge.net/* for details.

k3b [*options*]

k3b is a CD burning program with a graphical user interface. (For a command-line interface, see cdrecord.) Run the program and when the main window appears, visit the File menu. Browse to New Project and select the type of disc you want to burn. A New Data Project simply burns files and directories to the disc so it can be read on other computers. New Music Project and New Video Project should be self-explanatory. Once you've selected the type of project, drag your desired files or folders from the top half of the window (showing your filesystem) to the bottom half (listing what will be burned). When done, click the Burn icon.

The Tools menu also has useful commands. These include copying discs, working with ISO images, and ripping audio and video discs to files.

Video

mplayer	Video file playback.
gxine	Simple DVD player.
kino	Video editor.
HandBrake	Video ripper.

Linux has some fine programs for common video operations, such as playback, editing, and ripping. We'll briefly survey a few popular ones.

---

mplayer   stdin   stdout   -file   -- opt   --help   --version

mplayer [*options*] *video_files*...

The mplayer command plays video files in many formats: MPEG, AVI, MOV, and more:

    $ mplayer myfile.avi

While the video is playing, press the space bar to pause and resume, the cursor keys to jump forward and backward in time, and Q to quit. The program has dozens of options on its manpage, and you can learn more at *http://www.mplayerhq.hu*.

Other popular video players for Linux include vlc (*http://www.videolan.org/vlc/*), kaffeine (*http://kaffeine.kde.org/*), and xine (*http://sourceforge.net/projects/xine/*).

---

gxine   stdin   stdout   -file   -- opt   --help   --version

gxine [*options*] [*source*]

The gxine command displays a graphical video player that supports DVDs and video files. Just type gxine to get started with the graphical user interface, or provide a video source such as a file:

    $ gxine myfile.mpeg

or a Media Resource Locator (MRL):

    $ gxine dvd://home/jsmith/myvideo.iso

---

kino   stdin   stdout   -file   -- opt   --help   --version

kino [*file*]

kino is a video editor that can split videos into parts and reassemble them in another order. It can also capture video (if you have compatible hardware) and play it back. An overview of kino and video editing is beyond the scope of this book, so visit *http://kinodv.org/* for full details.

HandBrake   stdin   stdout   -file   -- opt   **--help**   --version

ghb [*options*]

HandBrakeCLI [*options*] -i *device* -o *file*

HandBrake is a video ripper (transcoder) that can copy video from DVDs and Blu-ray discs to files, as long as the discs are not copy-protected. It comes as a graphical program, ghb, and a

---

command-line program, `HandBrakeCLI` (note the capital letters, unusual for a Linux command). To get started, we recommend `ghb`. Full details can be found at *http://handbrake.fr*.

Installing Software

You will probably want to add further software to your Linux system from time to time. The method of installation varies, however, because Linux has multiple standards for "packaged" software. Your distro might do installations on the command line, with one or more GUI tools, or both. The most common package types are:

*.deb files
> Debian packages, used by Debian, Ubuntu, and other distros. We'll cover the package manager `aptitude` for installing software in this format.

*.rpm files
> RPM Package Manager files are used by Red Hat, Fedora, CentOS, and other distros. These are installed by the package managers `yum`, `rpm`, and on older systems, `up2date`.

*.tar.gz files, *.tar.Z files, and *.tar.bz2 files
> Compressed tar files. This kind of file isn't an installable "package" but a collection of files created by `tar` and compressed with `gzip` (*.gz*), `bzip2` (*.bz2*), or `compress` (.Z). Whereas Debian and RPM packages can be installed with a single command, compressed tar files usually require multiple manual steps.

You must learn which package type is used by your Linux system. In general, you cannot (or should not) mix package types like Debian and RPM. Fortunately, modern Linux systems are usually set up with a package manager when initially installed, so all you need to do is use it.

Most new software must be installed by the superuser, so you'll need to run the `su` command (or equivalent) before installation. For example:

```
$ su -l
Password: ********
# rpm -ivh mypackage.rpm
...etc...
```

or with sudo:

```
$ sudo rpm -ivh mypackage.rpm
Password: ********
```

To locate new software, run the "search" utility of your package manager, check your Linux DVDs or CD-ROMs, or visit fine sites like these:

http://freecode.com/
http://freshrpms.net/
http://rpmfusion.org/
http://sourceforge.net/

---

yum   stdin   **stdout**   - file   -- opt   **--help**   **--version**

yum [*options*] [*packages*]

yum is a popular package manager for RPM packages (*.rpm* files) found on Red Hat Enterprise Linux, Fedora, CentOS, and other distros. It is primarily a command-line tool, though you may encounter graphical front-ends for yum, such as PackageKit on Fedora Linux.

The following table lists common operations with yum. For operations on local files, which yum does not provide, we use the rpm command directly.

Action	yum command
Search for a package that meets your needs (supports wildcards * and ?).	yum search command_name
Check if a package is installed.	yum list installed *package_name*
Download a package but don't install it. This requires installing the downloadonly plugin first by running: yum install yum-downloadonly	yum --downloadonly install *package_name*

Action	yum command
Download and install a package.	yum install *package_name*
Install a package file.	rpm -ivh *package.rpm*
Learn about a package.	yum info *package_name*
List the contents of a package.	rpm -ql *package_name*
Discover which package an installed file belongs to.	yum provides */path/to/file*
Update an installed package.	yum update *package_name*
Remove an installed package.	yum remove *package_name*
List all packages installed on the system.	yum list installed | less
Check for updates for all packages on the system.	yum check-update
Update all packages on the system.	yum update

---

rpm   stdin   **stdout**   - file   -- opt   **--help**   **--version**

rpm [*options*] [*files*]

If you prefer to download and install RPM packages by hand, use rpm, the same package-management program that yum runs behind the scenes. Unlike yum, rpm works locally on your computer: it does not search software archives on the Internet for new packages.

rpm not only installs the software, but also makes sure your system has all prerequisites. For example, if package *superstuff* requires package *otherstuff* that you haven't installed, rpm will not install *superstuff*. If your system passes the test, however, rpm completely installs the software.

RPM filenames typically have the form *name-version.architec ture*.rpm. For example, *emacs-23.1-17.i386.rpm* indicates the emacs package, version 23.1-17, for i386 (Intel 80386 and higher) machines. Be aware that rpm sometimes requires a filename argument (like *emacs-23.1-17.i386.rpm*) and other times just the package name (like *emacs*).

Action	rpm command
Check if a package is installed	`rpm -q package_name`
Install a package file	`rpm -ivh package_file.rpm`
Learn about a package	`rpm -qi package_name`
List the contents of a package	`rpm -ql package_name`
Discover which package an installed file belongs to	`rpm -qf /path/to/file`
Update an installed package	`rpm -Uvh package_file.rpm`
Remove an installed package	`rpm -e package_name`
List all packages installed on the system	`rpm -qa	less`

aptitude   stdin **stdout** -file -- opt **--help** **--version**

`aptitude [options] [packages]`

aptitude is a package manager for the command line that manipu-lates Debian (*.deb*) packages. Some older Debian package manag-ers, including Advanced Packaging Tool (the `apt-get` command suite) and dpkg, are also in wide use today. (In our table of com-mands, we'll use dpkg to work with local files, since aptitude does not do this.) You'll also encounter graphical package managers like synaptic and Ubuntu's update-manager.

Action	yum command
Search for a package that meets your needs	`aptitude search package_name`
Check if a package is installed (examine the output for "State: not installed" or "State: installed")	`aptitude show package_name`
Download a package but don't in-stall it	`aptitude download package_name`
Download and install a package	`aptitude install package_name`
Install a package file	`dpkg -i package_file.deb`
Learn about a package	`aptitude show package_name`
List the contents of a package	`dpkg -L package_name`

Action	yum command
Discover which package an installed file belongs to	dpkg -S /path/to/file
Update an installed package	aptitude safe-upgrade package_name
Remove an installed package	aptitude remove package_name
List all packages installed on the system	aptitude search '~i' | less
Check for updates for all packages on the system	aptitude --simulate full-upgrade
Update all packages on the system	aptitude full-upgrade

---

tar.gz and tar.bz2 Files

Packaged software files with names ending *.tar.gz* and *.tar.bz2* typically contain source code that you'll need to compile (build) before installation. Typical build instructions are:

1. List the package contents, one file per line. Assure yourself that each file, when extracted, won't overwrite something precious on your system, either accidentally or maliciously:[21]

   ```
   $ tar tvzf package.tar.gz | less      For gzip files
   $ tar tvjf package.tar.bz2 | less      For bzip2 files
   ```

2. If satisfied, extract the files into a new directory. Run these commands as yourself, not as root, for safety reasons:

   ```
   $ mkdir newdir
   $ cd newdir
   $ tar xvzf <path>/package.tar.gz      For gzip files
   $ tar xvjf <path>/package.tar.bz2      For bzip2 files
   ```

3. Look for an extracted file named *INSTALL* or *README*. Read it to learn how to build the software, for example:

   ```
   $ cd newdir
   $ less INSTALL
   ```

21. A maliciously designed tar file could include an absolute file path like */etc/passwd* designed to overwrite your system password file.

4. Usually the *INSTALL* or *README* file will tell you to run a script called `configure` in the current directory, then run `make`, then run `make install`. Examine the options you may pass to the `configure` script:

```
$ ./configure --help
```

Then install the software:

```
$ ./configure options
$ make
$ su
Password: *******
# make install
```

Programming with Shell Scripts

Earlier when we covered the shell (bash), we said it had a programming language built in. In fact, you can write programs, or *shell scripts*, to accomplish tasks that a single command cannot. Like any good programming language, the shell has variables, conditionals (if-then-else), loops, input and output, and more. Entire books have been written on shell scripting, so we'll be covering the bare minimum to get you started. For full documentation, run `info bash`, search the Web, or pick up a more in-depth O'Reilly book.

Whitespace and Linebreaks

`bash` shell scripts are very sensitive to whitespace and linebreaks. Because the "keywords" of this programming language are actually commands evaluated by the shell, you need to separate arguments with whitespace. Likewise, a linebreak in the middle of a command will mislead the shell into thinking the command is incomplete. Follow the conventions we present here and you should be fine.

If you must break a long command into multiple lines, end each line (except the last) with a single \ character, which means "continued on next line":

```
$ grep abcdefghijklmnopqrstuvwxyz file1 file2 \
file3 file4
```

Variables

We described shell variables earlier:

```
$ MYVAR=6
$ echo $MYVAR
6
```

All values held in variables are strings, but if they are numeric, the shell will treat them as numbers when appropriate.

```
$ NUMBER="10"
$ expr $NUMBER + 5
15
```

When you refer to a variable's value in a shell script, it's a good idea to surround it with double quotes to prevent certain runtime errors. An undefined variable, or a variable with spaces in its value, will evaluate to something unexpected if not surrounded by quotes, causing your script to malfunction.

```
$ FILENAME="My Document"               Space in the name
$ ls $FILENAME                         Try to list it
ls: My: No such file or directory      Oops! ls saw 2 arguments
ls: Document: No such file or directory
$ ls -l "$FILENAME"                    List it properly
My Document                            ls saw only 1 argument
```

If a variable name is evaluated adjacent to another string, surround it with curly braces to prevent unexpected behavior:

```
$ HAT="fedora"
$ echo "The plural of $HAT is $HATs"
The plural of fedora is                Oops! No variable "HATs"
$ echo  "The plural of $HAT is ${HAT}s"
The plural of fedora is fedoras        What we wanted
```

Input and Output

Script output is provided by the echo and printf commands, which we described in "Screen Output" on page 168:

```
$ echo "Hello world"
Hello world
$ printf "I am %d years old\n" `expr 20 + 20`
I am 40 years old
```

Input is provided by the **read** command, which reads one line from standard input and stores it in a variable:

```
$ read name
Sandy Smith <ENTER>
$ echo "I read the name $name"
I read the name Sandy Smith
```

Booleans and Return Codes

Before we can describe conditionals and loops, we need to explain the concept of a Boolean (true/false) test. To the shell, the value 0 means true or success, and anything else means false or failure. (Think of zero as "no error" and other values as error codes.)

Additionally, every Linux command returns an integer value, called a *return code* or *exit status*, to the shell when the command exits.

You can see this value in the special variable $?:

```
$ cat myfile
My name is Sandy Smith and
I really like Ubuntu Linux
$ grep Smith myfile
My name is Sandy Smith and        A match was found...
$ echo $?
0                                 ...so return code is "success"
$ grep aardvark myfile
$ echo $?                         No match was found...
1                                 ...so return code is "failure"
```

The return codes of a command are usually documented on its manpage.

test and "["

The `test` command (built into the shell) will evaluate simple Boolean expressions involving numbers and strings, setting its exit status to 0 (true) or 1 (false):

```
$ test 10 -lt 5        Is 10 less than 5?
$ echo $?
1                      No, it isn't
$ test -n "hello"      Does the string "hello" have nonzero length?
$ echo $?
0                      Yes, it does
```

Here are common `test` arguments for checking properties of integers, strings, and files:

File tests

-d *name*	File *name* is a directory
-f *name*	File *name* is a regular file
-L *name*	File *name* is a symbolic link
-r *name*	File *name* exists and is readable
-w *name*	File *name* exists and is writable
-x *name*	File *name* exists and is executable
-s *name*	File *name* exists and its size is nonzero
f1 -nt *f2*	File *f1* is newer than file *f2*
f1 -ot *f2*	File *f1* is older than file *f2*

String tests

s1 = *s2*	String *s1* equals string *s2*
s1 != *s2*	String *s1* does not equal string *s2*
-z *s1*	String *s1* has zero length
-n *s1*	String *s1* has nonzero length

Numeric tests

a -eq *b*	Integers *a* and *b* are equal
a -ne *b*	Integers *a* and *b* are not equal
a -gt *b*	Integer *a* is greater than integer *b*

a -ge *b*	Integer *a* is greater than or equal to integer *b*
a -lt *b*	Integer *a* is less than integer *b*
a -le *b*	Integer *a* is less than or equal to integer *b*

Combining and negating tests

t1 -a t2	And: Both tests t1 and t2 are true
t1 -o t2	Or: Either test t1 or t2 is true
! *your_test*	Negate the test, i.e., your_test is false
\(*your_test* \)	Parentheses are used for grouping, as in algebra

test has an unusual alias, "[" (left square bracket), as a shorthand for use with conditionals and loops. If you use this shorthand, you must supply a final argument of "]" (right square
bracket) to signify the end of the test. The following tests are
identical to the previous two:

```
$ [ 10 -lt 5 ]
$ echo $?
1
$ [ -n "hello" ]
$ echo $?
0
```

Remember that "[" is a command like any other, so it is followed by *individual arguments separated by whitespace*. So if
you mistakenly forget some whitespace:

```
$ [ 5 -lt 4]          No space between 4 and ]
bash: [: missing ']'
```

then test thinks the final argument is the string "4]" and com-
plains that the final bracket is missing.

true and false

bash has built-in commands **true** and **false**, which simply set
their exit status to 0 and 1, respectively.

```
$ true
$ echo $?
0
$ false
```

```
$ echo $?
1
```

These will be useful when we discuss conditionals and loops.

Conditionals

The `if` statement chooses between alternatives, each of which
may have a complex test. The simplest form is the `if-then`
statement:

```
if command              If exit status of command is 0
then
   body
fi
```

For example:

```
if [ `whoami` = "root" ]
then
   echo "You are the superuser"
fi
```

Next is the `if-then-else` statement:

```
if command
then
   body1
else
   body2
fi
```

For example:

```
if [ `whoami` = "root" ]
then
   echo "You are the superuser"
else
   echo "You are an ordinary dude"
fi
```

Finally, we have the form `if-then-elif-else`, which may have
as many tests as you like:

```
if command1
then
   body1
elif command2
```

```
then
  body2
elif ...
  ...
else
  bodyN
fi
```

For example:

```
if [ `whoami` = "root" ]
then
  echo "You are the superuser"
elif [ "$USER" = "root" ]
then
  echo "You might be the superuser"
elif [ "$bribe" -gt 10000 ]
then
  echo "You can pay to be the superuser"
else
  echo "You are still an ordinary dude"
fi
```

The **case** statement evaluates a single value and branches to an appropriate piece of code:

```
echo "What would you like to do?"
read answer
case "$answer" in
  eat)
    echo "OK, have a hamburger"
    ;;
  sleep)
    echo "Good night then"
    ;;
  *)
    echo "I'm not sure what you want to do"
    echo "I guess I'll see you tomorrow"
    ;;
esac
```

The general form is:

```
case string in
  expr1)
    body1
    ;;
  expr2)
```

```
  body2
  ;;
...
exprN)
  bodyN
  ;;
*)
  bodyelse
  ;;
esac
```

where *string* is any value, usually a variable value like $myvar, and *expr1* through *exprN* are patterns (run the command `info bash reserved case` for details), with the final * like a final "else." Each set of commands must be terminated by ;; (as shown):

```
case $letter in
  X)
    echo "$letter is an X"
    ;;
  [aeiou])
    echo "$letter is a vowel"
    ;;
  [0-9])
    echo "$letter is a digit, silly"
    ;;
  *)
    echo "The letter '$letter' is not supported"
    ;;
esac
```

Loops

The `while` loop repeats a set of commands as long as a condition is true.

```
while command          While the exit status of command is 0
do
  body
done
```

For example, if this is the script `myscript`:

```
i=0
while [ $i -lt 3 ]
```

```
do
  echo "$i"
  i=`expr $i + 1`
done

$ ./myscript
0
1
2
```

The **until** loop repeats until a condition becomes true:

```
until command          While the exit status of command is nonzero
do
  body
done
```

For example:

```
i=0
until [ $i -ge 3 ]
do
  echo "$i"
  i=`expr $i + 1`
done

$ ./myscript
0
1
2
```

The **for** loop iterates over values from a list:

```
for variable in list
do
  body
done
```

For example:

```
for name in Tom Jack Harry
do
  echo "$name is my friend"
done
$ ./myscript
Tom is my friend
Jack is my friend
Harry is my friend
```

The **for** loop is particularly handy for processing lists of files; for example, all files of a certain type in the current directory:

```
for file in *.doc *.docx
do
  echo "$file is a stinky Microsoft Word file"
done
```

Be careful to avoid infinite loops, using **while** with the condition **true**, or **until** with the condition **false**:

```
while true          Beware: infinite loop!
do
  echo "forever"
done

until false         Beware: infinite loop!
do
  echo "forever again"
done
```

Use **break** or **exit** to terminate these loops based on some condition inside their bodies.

Break and Continue

The **break** command jumps out of the nearest enclosing loop. Consider this simple script called **myscript**:

```
for name in Tom Jack Harry
do
  echo $name
  echo "again"
done
echo "all done"

$ ./myscript
Tom
again
Jack
again
Harry
again
all done
```

Now with a break:

```
for name in Tom Jack Harry
do
  echo $name
  if [ "$name" = "Jack" ]
  then
    break
  fi
  echo "again"
done
echo "all done"

$ ./myscript
Tom
again
Jack            The break occurs after this line
all done
```

The continue command forces a loop to jump to its next iteration.

```
for name in Tom Jack Harry
do
  echo $name
  if [ "$name" = "Jack" ]
  then
    continue
  fi
  echo "again"
done
echo "all done"

$ ./myscript
Tom
again
Jack            The continue occurs after this line
Harry
again
all done
```

break and continue also accept a numeric argument (break *N*, continue *N*) to control multiple layers of loops (e.g., jump out of *N* layers of loops), but this kind of scripting leads to spaghetti code and we don't recommend it.

Creating and Running Shell Scripts

To create a shell script, simply put bash commands into a file as you would type them. To run the script, you have three choices:

Prepend #!/bin/bash *and make the file executable*
> This is the most common way to run scripts. Add the line:
>
> ```
> #!/bin/bash
> ```
>
> to the very top of the script file. It must be the first line of the file, left-justified. Then make the file executable:
>
> ```
> $ chmod +x myscript
> ```
>
> Optionally, move it into a directory in your search path. Then run it like any other command:
>
> ```
> $ myscript
> ```
>
> If the script is in your current directory, but the current directory "." is not in your search path, you'll need to prepend "./" so the shell finds the script:
>
> ```
> $ ./myscript
> ```
>
> The current directory is generally not in your search path for security reasons. (You wouldn't want a local script named (say) "ls" to override the real **ls** command.)

Pass to bash
> bash will interpret its argument as the name of a script and run it.
>
> ```
> $ bash myscript
> ```

Run in current shell with "." or source
> The preceding methods run your script as an independent entity that has no effect on your current shell.[22] If you want your script to make changes to your current shell (setting variables, changing directory, and so on), it can

---

22. That's because the script runs in a separate shell (a *subshell* or *child shell*) that cannot alter the original shell.

be run in the current shell with the source or "." command:

```
$ . myscript
$ source myscript
```

Command-Line Arguments

Shell scripts can accept command-line arguments and options just like other Linux commands. (In fact, some common Linux commands *are* scripts.) Within your shell script, you can refer to these arguments as $1, $2, $3, and so on.

```
$ cat myscript
#!/bin/bash
echo "My name is $1 and I come from $2"

$ ./myscript Johnson Wisconsin
My name is Johnson and I come from Wisconsin
$ ./myscript Bob
My name is Bob and I come from
```

Your script can test the number of arguments it received with $#:

```
if [ $# -lt 2 ]
then
  echo "$0 error: you must supply two arguments"
else
  echo "My name is $1 and I come from $2"
fi
```

The special value $0 contains the name of the script, and is handy for usage and error messages:

```
$ ./myscript Bob
./myscript error: you must supply two arguments
```

To iterate over all command-line arguments, use a for loop with the special variable $@, which holds all arguments:

```
for arg in $@
do
  echo "I found the argument $arg"
done
```

Exiting with a Return Code

The exit command terminates your script and passes a given return code to the shell. By tradition, scripts should return 0 for success and 1 (or other nonzero value) on failure. If your script doesn't call exit, the return code is automatically 0.

```
if [ $# -lt 2 ]
then
  echo "$0 error: you must supply two arguments"
  exit 1
else
  echo "My name is $1 and I come from $2"
fi
exit 0

$ ./myscript Bob
./myscript error: you must supply two arguments
$ echo $?
1
```

Beyond Shell Scripting

Shell scripts are fine for many purposes, but Linux comes with much more powerful scripting languages, as well as compiled programming languages. Here are a few.

Language	Program	To get started...
C, C++	gcc, g++	man gcc
		http://www.gnu.org/software/gcc/
.NET	mono	man mono
		http://www.mono-project.com/
Java	javac	*http://java.sun.com/*
Perl	perl	man perl
		http://www.perl.com/
PHP	php	man php
		http://www.php.net/
Python	python	man python

Language	Program	To get started...
		http://www.python.org/
Ruby	ruby	*http://ruby-lang.org/*

Final Words

Although we've covered many commands and capabilities of Linux, we've just scratched the surface. Most distributions come with *thousands* of other programs. We encourage you to continue reading, exploring, and learning the capabilities of your Linux systems. Good luck!

Acknowledgments

I am very grateful to the many readers who purchased the first edition of this book, making the second edition possible. My heartfelt thanks also go to my long-time editor Mike Loukides and new editor Andy Oram, the O'Reilly production staff, the technical review team (Stephen Figgins, Stephen Roylance, and Ellen Siever), Chris Connors at Vistaprint, and as always, my wonderful family, Lisa and Sophia.

Index

We'd like to hear your suggestions for improving our indexes. Send email to
index@oreilly.com.

xxdiff command, 98

Y

Z

Get even more for your money.

Join the O'Reilly Community, and register the O'Reilly books you own. It's free, and you'll get:

- $4.99 ebook upgrade offer
- 40% upgrade offer on O'Reilly print books
- Membership discounts on books and events
- Free lifetime updates to ebooks and videos
- Multiple ebook formats, DRM FREE
- Participation in the O'Reilly community
- Newsletters
- Account management
- 100% Satisfaction Guarantee

Registering your books is easy:
1. Go to: oreilly.com/go/register
2. Create an O'Reilly login.
3. Provide your address.
4. Register your books.

Note: English-language books only

To order books online:
oreilly.com/store

For questions about products or an order:
orders@oreilly.com

To sign up to get topic-specific email announcements and/or news about upcoming books, conferences, special offers, and new technologies:
elists@oreilly.com

For technical questions about book content:
booktech@oreilly.com

To submit new book proposals to our editors:
proposals@oreilly.com

O'Reilly books are available in multiple DRM-free ebook formats. For more information:
oreilly.com/ebooks

O'REILLY®

Spreading the knowledge of innovators   oreilly.com

The information you need, when and where you need it.

With Safari Books Online, you can:

Access the contents of thousands of technology and business books

- Quickly search over 7000 books and certification guides
- Download whole books or chapters in PDF format, at no extra cost, to print or read on the go
- Copy and paste code
- Save up to 35% on O'Reilly print books
- **New!** Access mobile-friendly books directly from cell phones and mobile devices

Stay up-to-date on emerging topics before the books are published

- Get on-demand access to evolving manuscripts.
- Interact directly with authors of upcoming books

Explore thousands of hours of video on technology and design topics

- Learn from expert video tutorials
- Watch and replay recorded conference sessions

O'REILLY®

Spreading the knowledge of innovators   oreilly.com

CPSIA information can be obtained at www.ICGtesting.com
Printed in the USA
BVOW11n0852280214

346259BV00004B/4/P